How to
Read
Poetry
Like a
Professor

How to
Read
Poetry
Like a
Professor

A Quippy and Sonorous
Guide to Verse

Thomas C. Foster

HARPER ● PERENNIAL

NEW YORK • LONDON • TORONTO • SYDNEY • NEW DELHI • AUCKLAND

HARPER ⬤ **PERENNIAL**

Copyright and permission notices continued on page 211.

FIRST EDITION

Designed by Jamie Lynn Kerner

Library of Congress Cataloging-in-Publication Data has been applied for.

ISBN 978-0-06-211378-8

18 19 20 21 22   LSC   10 9 8 7 6 5 4 3 2 1

For Leonora H. Smith, F. Richard Thomas, and Danny Rendleman
Superb poets, better friends

Contents

What
Is
Poetry?

Introduction

A (Slightly) Alien Life-Form

E VERYBODY TALKS ABOUT POETRY, BUT NOBODY DOES ANYTHING about it. Or maybe that's the weather. Actually, one of the problems with poetry is that people don't talk about it. Or not enough. In part, we don't know what to say. Maybe it's just intimidation. I can't tell you the number of students over the years who told me that they like to write poems, but they don't read them. Seems a little one-sided, doesn't it? And if you don't read them, how do you even know the stuff you're writing is poetry? This suggests an impulse toward poetry is strong in a lot of us, including some who don't much like it. But we already knew that; the modern American poet Marianne Moore said of poetry, "I, too, dislike it." In a poem, no less. Called "Poetry." Of course it was.

I think that for most people, however, the matter isn't so much not liking poetry as feeling somehow overmatched, as if it were a contest and the other side had better equipment and more skill. Or as more than one student has said to me over the years, "I like poetry, but I don't understand it." Not an enviable position in which to find oneself. I actually think a more accurate second half of that statement would be something closer to "I don't understand it *enough*." The truth is that at least in my experience readers mostly understand the poems they read. They will get the gist of the poem, especially if the poem is written in their own idiom. If you're reading Shakespeare's Elizabethan English or Geoffrey Chaucer's Middle English, there are nearly insurmountable barriers to understanding for a lot of folks before we ever get to the poetry part. But almost anyone can read a lot of contemporary poetry, can take plenty away from Adrienne Rich or Billy Collins or any of a hundred recent poets who intend to be understood. And there are lots and lots of them. Honest.

What we need, then, isn't basic literacy skills (although possessing those is an excellent beginning) but the specialized set of tools for dealing with poetry. After all, who wants to spend the time reading something only to *mostly* understand it? Let's begin to fill that toolbox.

The learning-to-read-poetry story—or, for me, the learning-to-teach-how-to-read-poetry story—came when I would teach our course in the classics in translation, or what we called, immodestly, "The Literature of Greece and Rome." The syllabus wound up considerably smaller than the grandiose title suggests, focusing on *The Iliad*, *The Aeneid*, and the three "Theban" plays by Sophocles about Oedipus and his dysfunctional family. We would start with the oldest work, Homer's great epic about the wrath of Achilles. And here, the non-majors had an advantage. The English department evidently did an excellent job teaching its students to expect all sorts of hidden meanings and subtle uses of language in poetry, because our majors, confronted with a massive narrative poem, drove themselves crazy trying to figure out why, as more than one of them asked me, in a certain spot Homer refers to Hector "of the shining helm," in another as "giant, man-slaughtering" Hector or some other formulaic device. And they hated my answer: because in the original Greek those words fit the line. See, here's the thing. *The Iliad* is somewhere around twenty-one thousand lines long. It was composed over a period of centuries as it was handed down from singer to singer ("Homer" is a convenient

fiction for discussing the tradition of this great poem and its only sur-
viving companion, *The Odyssey*) and never written down until well
after the time of its composition. It was performed before a live studio
audience as an oral recitation. In all oral narrative poetry—usually
called *oral-formulaic* verse—not only the length of the lines but also
the rhythmic pattern of the lines is dictated absolutely. We'll talk later
about how that works, but for now, you just need to understand that
if you had, say, a six-syllable hole in your line and the syllables had to
sound "DUM-da-dum, DUM-da-dum," with a strong stress on the
first syllable followed by two unstressed syllables, and "giant, man-
slaughtering Hector" (in Greek, remember) was not going to fill the
bill, then you needed to go with "Hector of the shining helm" instead.
Those descriptive phrases are what we call the *formulas*, and the
singer might have a half dozen of them for each major character. This
reservoir of formulas was really helpful if, at line 18,699, you lost your
place and had to get back on track; you had only to pull out "patient,
long-suffering Odysseus" and by the end of the line you were once
more in rhythm. Never mind that Odysseus has no need of being ei-
ther patient or long-suffering until the sequel, when he will take ten
years getting home. The casual visitors didn't have much trouble with
this context, but the majors would spend most of the epic looking for
the secret motivation the poet had for using this particular formula.
Sometimes, a little learning is a damnable nuisance.

SINCE I FIRST PUBLISHED *HOW TO READ LITERATURE LIKE A PROFES-
SOR* back in 2003, there has been a faint but steady drumbeat of—
what?—not exactly criticism or complaint. Something more like
pleading. It goes like this: "That's all great, but it's mostly about stories
and novels, and what I don't understand (and would really like to)
is poetry." I heard this especially a few years later when the genre-
specific *How to Read Novels Like a Professor* came out: "Okay, fine,
but what about poetry?" This is hardly surprising. It is possible to get
through a fairly decent teacher-training English program with min-

imal contact with poetry, which strategy may seem the safe bet for students who want to avoid stumbling over this genre they really don't understand, but it can be a major liability out in the teaching profession. If the program requires a course in nineteenth-century American literature, for instance, it may be possible to avoid the survey of American Romanticism or Realism, either of which would involve poetry, and instead take a course in nineteenth-century American novels or a major-figures course in, say, Mark Twain and Henry James. I saw those choices made many times while advising students. What that means, though, is that the student missed Emerson and Longfellow or Whitman and Dickinson, all of whom are fairly major figures in American letters. Taken to its logical (or maybe illogical) extreme, what happens is that the only serious poet the students study is Shakespeare, whose work is not inclined to induce a high comfort level with poetry. Could be worse, of course. Could be Milton or Spenser. At least Shakespeare figures prominently in the secondary curriculum. So we in the university community often send our aspiring teachers out into battle woefully underprepared to address poetry. And they often know they're not ready. And they're scared.

Come on! It doesn't have to be this hard.

First of all, poetry can be a lot of fun. It can be tender, funny, satiric, erotic, lovely, or pretty much any other thing a human being can be. I know of a poem in which the speaker of the poem is confronted by a wife who, frustrated that her husband routinely spends too much time at the pub, compares herself to glass of beer. It's the sexiest glass of beer ever. What's not to like? And beyond that, there are lots of poems that we can read with no problem once we take down that barrier of defensiveness that we set up when we fear that we may not be up to the job. Beyond that, poetry offers a window into the human experience. The great poets make statements about the emotional and psychological heavy lifting that poetry undertakes, as when the verse playwright Christopher Fry says that "poetry is the language by which man explores his own amazement." That's what we want, right? Love, hate, envy, elation, dejection, gentleness, the mysteries of life and death, handled in a small package.

We'll look at various definitions and descriptions of poetry in a bit, but I want to offer a partial one preemptively: **Poetry uses language to take us to a place beyond language.** I could say that it is the place where one soul meets with another, but that's a little mystical for this discussion. Perhaps that's what alarms readers, whichever way we describe it. Both the meeting of souls and the inherent self-contradiction of language going to a place beyond itself can sound pretentious, at best. But they are also what make poetry so exciting, allowing us to go to intellectual or psychic spaces that we can't ordinarily access. Besides, a touch of terror adds piquancy to our excitement.

As we move along in this discussion, I want you to keep in mind something most people intuit even if they can't articulate it: **Reading poetry requires more than just your brain.** Writing poetry is a full-contact activity; so, too, must we bring our entire being to bear on the act of reading it. That is certainly a part of the intimidation that we may feel when we launch into a book of poems, the sense that demands being made on us are of a different order than those made by our other reading. Historian David McCullough and poet Seamus Heaney are giants in their fields, but a McCullough biography—*Truman*, say, or *John Adams*—asks very different things of its readers than Heaney's volumes of verse *North* or *Field Work*, however much those may be informed by history. We assume going into the former that we will learn things; we know (and maybe occasionally dread) going into the latter that we will be changed. That's okay, though. Change is good.

PERILS AND ANXIETIES

IF THOSE ARE the positives that poems can offer us, what are the negatives? Because you know in your bones they exist. The basic problem that readers have with poetry is that they don't know what to do with it: "How does it work? What are the rules? I know there's an iambic something or other, but I don't know how it works. And why does it have to look so funny?" Herewith, a small sampling of our issues with literature in verse:

- Poems don't look like other forms of writing.
- Poems obey unfamiliar rules that other writing doesn't have. And we don't know what they are.
- There are all these weird terms and jargon that we don't encounter anywhere else. And some of them are foreign: "tetrameter," "scansion," "prosody," "terza rima," "iamb," "trochee," "stanza." Who needs that?
- What do we do about rhythm? Is it like songs or rap or what? And rhyme, for that matter?
- Sometimes lines don't make sense when we read them.
- How come words are out of order sometimes?

Ever heard any of those? Or thought them? Or said them? Yep, me, too.

WHAT'S IN IT FOR YOU?

I IMAGINE YOU want to be able to confront a new poem, one you've never seen before, and not feel a sick knot forming in your stomach. Instead, you want to be able to think, I can do this, and I know what to do with this.

- The first thing we want to accomplish is the very basic reading activity of being able to receive the primary meaning of the poem we've just met.
- You will learn to account for those technical elements that made your eyelids heavy in English class (meter, diction,

rhyme, line structures—length, order, regularity) and to see them as allies in reading for meaning and pleasure.

- We will work on listening for those secondary meanings by paying attention to the echoes that the language of poetry summons up.

- Every genre has its own grammar, by which I mean a set of rules and practices by which the genre achieves meaning and works its magic. We will explore the grammar that operates in poetry so that we can better understand how poems are made—and what we can make out of them.

- Together, we will break down that defensive wall that we erect against this thing that we don't understand. Or entirely trust.

- We will look at a wide variety of poems. Most will be in English, because few things lose as much in translation as poetry. Some will be quite old. But still great. Besides, if someone can rap the opening of Chaucer's *Canterbury Tales* (and people have), we ought to be able to get with older material, too. It's really hard to talk about poetry in English and skip the name brands—Shakespeare's *Hamlet* and a sonnet or two, Samuel Taylor Coleridge's "Kubla Khan" and "The Rime of the Ancient Mariner," Walt Whitman's *Leaves of Grass*, Poe's "The Raven,"—but we will also want poems in a more modern idiom from Edna St. Vincent Millay to E. E. Cummings to Billy Collins to Seamus Heaney. And maybe a couple of poets you thought were only songwriters.

And we'll do all this while having as much fun as we can while doing work. Seriously (and I don't plan to be serious very often from this point on), if we can't have a good time horsing around with poems, what's the point? Besides, it isn't really work; it's really just a lovely form of play. That sometimes rhymes.

Shall we begin?

1

The Sounds of Sense

ONE OF THE PROBLEMS THAT NEWCOMERS—AND SOMETIMES NOT-so-new-comers—to poetry have is that they believe that they don't know how to read a poem. Is it in your language or not? I don't know how to read a poem in French, but that's because my French is so degraded with disuse that I can't read *anything* in it. In English, on the other hand, I'm mostly competent, and so are you. Look at it this way: you've been reading in your native language almost your whole life and been hearing and speaking it even longer. A poem is an act of written communication. Like almost all such acts, it is written in sentences. I can't stress this enough: virtually all poems are written in sentences. Lines—maybe, maybe not. Sentences, almost definitely. Which are the basic unit of meaning in the mother tongue. So there is a policy to follow: read the sentences.

Yeah, but those sentences are different. You know, more, well, poetic.

I think what you mean is that they can be more compressed or that word order is sometimes inverted, which can throw us off. The flow of words can feel different in some poems, especially older ones. That about the size of it?

Sure, something like that.

Okay, you've just located one thing that makes poetry in English a challenge: the language is fairly flexible in terms of the order in which words can be placed in a sentence. Not like Latin, where the verb always showed up at the end. Still, for a sentence to make sense, that order can't be pushed beyond certain boundaries. Consider the first sentence of this paragraph, for instance. If I rearrange the clause after the colon, I can't, for instance, say, "The language is fairly flexible *can be placed* in terms of the order in which words in a sentence." To do so is to render it not only meaningless but also sort of anti-meaning. The verb phrase "can be placed" wrecks the meaning of "fairly flexible" and, worse than that, seems (falsely) to lead into "in terms of the order," which only leads to confusion. Not only that, but without them, "which words in a sentence" becomes a sort of promissory note for a meaning that never occurs. No, those three italicized words have only one possible position, and that is between the two prepositional phrases: "in which words can be placed in a sentence." It won't matter whether the sentence occurs in prose or poetry: that word order must be what it is. Words, then, may get slightly rearranged in a poem, but only within limits. *So the basic concept remains intact: read from a capital letter to the first following period, observing all speed limits and sign posts.*

Contained in that edict are three rules:

Rule One: Read the words. That seems straightforward enough, but it can be tricky, as we shall see.

Rule Two: Read ALL the words. The only way to guarantee this one is to read the poem in a way that won't let you skip any words or substitute words not there for those that are. And for most beginning readers of poetry—heck, for most experienced readers, too—that means reading the poem aloud. We'll come back to that one.

Rule Three: Read sentences. I won't deny that this practice is made slightly more difficult when the poem capitalizes the first letter of each line. Or when a latter-day poet like W. S. Merwin abjures both capital letters and punctuation (including periods), relying instead on line length and rhythm for meaning units. Merwin is a rarity, if a wondrous one, so we'll dispense with him for the moment. Just know that he is out there. In the other instance, the only real solution is to notice which capital letter matters, the one right after a period, and to do your best to ignore those others that signify nothing but the beginning of a line.

So, then, having raised the issue of lines, capitalized beginnings or not, I have to give you some incredibly annoying advice: pretend they're not there. Yeah, I know, that's like going to a basketball game and ignoring the basket. Lines are the most identifiable feature of a poem. In terms of meaning, however, they are rarely helpful and frequently counterproductive. Again, Merwin would be one of the rare exceptions. Let's make that **Rule Four: Ignore lines on first reading.** There, that makes things tricky. Read the words but ignore the lines that contain and organize them. No problem, right?

It is imperative that you learn to do so, however, because *lines are the enemies of meaning.* They make your eye stop when they end, at least for a moment, as it travels over the gap to the beginning of the next one. Their existence is so pronounced that it seems as if they should mean something on their own, which, once in a while, they do. And sometimes they end with some sort of punctuation, which means you have a shorter or longer pause; that's what I meant about speed limits and sign posts a little bit ago, which leads to **Rule Five: Obey all punctuation, including its absence.**

That doesn't seem so hard. I've been doing that ever since I learned to read.

I know you have, so tell me why students have so much trouble doing it with poems. I have heard students stop at every line-end, blow right through midline periods, completely ignore every comma, and pretty much do anything it is possible to do or not do with the marks and spaces that lie between words. Conceptually, it's a no-brainer, but those darned lines get in the way. So it requires new practice to follow the guideposts that you always have. Pause for commas. Pause more for colons, semicolons, and dashes. Stop for question marks, exclamation marks, and, of course, periods. And treat every punctuation mark exactly like every other one of its type no matter where it falls in the line, after line one, three, seven, ten, or twenty-two (and let's hope it never comes to that). The really big problem, however, comes not where there are marks but where there aren't. An unpunctuated line-end (called an enjambed line) should be treated as you treat every other unpunctuated space between words: keep going. It's the line thing, though. Sure, you have never regarded the space at the end of a line of prose as anything other than what it was. But lines are not structural elements in prose. In poetry, however, they are, and reading through them with some measure of smoothness takes some practice.

All of this is leading to something you probably don't want to hear: **Rule Six: Read the poem aloud.** This may be the most important rule of all. Why? Because if you're like most of us, you've never heard enough poems read aloud. Or, if you have, they may have been read very badly. Unless you've heard a poem by a practicing poet, which is to say the person who wrote it, that means that you have to learn to hear it by learning to speak it. Poet Robert Pinsky, in *The Sounds of Poetry*, says that poetry is a "vocal, which is to say a bodily, art." That is, he explains, that it is meant to be spoken and heard, which involves breath and vocal cords and diaphragms and eardrums, among other bits and pieces of the person. In speaking it and hearing it, we learn to *feel* poetry. Of course, there is that vibration of the eardrum that gets transmitted to tiny bones of the ear and on across nerves and synapses to the brain, the tightening in the chest or gut, the rising or falling sensation in the stomach, the hairs that stand up on arms or the back of the neck, the sense that the top of one's head, as Emily Dickinson said, is being removed. We have bodily as well as emotional or intellectual responses to poetry.

That may be an extreme case. Not every poem can have that head-blowing-up effect; if they all did, we would be forced to give up poetry entirely. But every poem read or heard registers something, even if that thing is only sound. Because sounds, as Mr. Pinsky insists, are not merely auditory, but also visceral.

And one last rule: **Read it again.** My friends in composition studies have a saying: "Writing is rewriting." I'm pretty sure one or two of them use it as their meditation mantra. The same is true of literary studies, especially in the case of poetry: **Reading is rereading.** You haven't begun to grasp a poem until you have read it a second time. This is a problem, naturally, if your poem is *Paradise Lost* or *Leaves of Grass*. But I'm willing to bet that's not a customary issue for poetry readers. Shorter is easier; sonnets are perfect for rereading, odes slightly harder, and so on. The point is that a first reading is so consumed with just navigating your way through (and putting the top of your head back on when it blows off), with just getting from *A* to *Z*, that a second pass is mandatory. For best results, I recommend taking a few minutes off between readings. Not enough time to forget this newly discovered territory, only to let it settle in a bit. Go make a cup of tea or build a sandwich. Let the dog out. Let the dog in. Reread. That's when you'll start making the poem your own.

What we're talking about in all of this is the "sound of sense," a term I have pilfered from Robert Frost. What he means is that a poem should and often does have a certain sound, a combination of rhythm and other aural elements, that convey a sense of what is being said. When it's done right, he elaborates, you can discern the general meaning of a conversation from behind a closed door—and remember that he was writing when doors were more solid and more sound-damping than most contemporary doors. Here's his example of a conversation that he invokes to illustrate his point:

> YOU MEAN TO TELL ME YOU CAN'T READ?
> I SAID NO SUCH THING.
>
> WELL, READ THEN.
> YOU'RE NOT MY TEACHER.

We understand what Frost means in large part because he chooses his example so well. We can "hear" the tone of each of those sentences, the incredulity of the question followed by the defensiveness of "I said no such thing," and the challenge in the injunction to read, which leads to more defensiveness. Further, we understand that, if we were over-hearing this conversation, even if we couldn't make out the words, we would nevertheless know what sort of dialogue was taking place. If we want further proof, we have only to read any of his poetic dialogues, where the sound-of-sense principle is on full display.

It is worth observing that this notion of the sound of sense is not inevitable. Frost notes that much prose (think institutional documents, among other sorts of lifeless writing) has sense without the sound of sense, while it is possible, as Lewis Carroll proves in the *Alice* books, to have the sound of sense while producing utter—and utterly delightful, in those cases—nonsense. For now, however, we should stick to the main point.

INTO PRACTICE: THE SOUNDS OF POEMS

LET'S TAKE THIS idea for a test drive. Here's the beginning of a deceptively simple poem by one of America's great poets:

> *Because I could not stop for Death –*
> *He kindly stopped for me –*
> *The Carriage held but just Ourselves –*
> *And Immortality.*

That's lovely, and maybe a little chilling. It's also Emily Dickinson (1830–1886), who didn't title her poems, so we know them by their first lines. And what does this first line say? "Because I could not stop for Death"—sounds like someone is pretty busy. Or had been. When "Death" comes to take you for a ride, your level of busyness goes down. His stopping is "kind" (good of him, don't you think?), and "He" will be marked by good behavior throughout. That last line brings us up a little short, as the ends of her stanzas often do, for "Immortality," while not an actual occupant in the carriage, is inevitable in the situation.

The following stanza amplifies the statements of the first:

> We slowly drove – He knew no haste
> And I had put away
> My labor and my leisure too,
> For His Civility –

If we think about this stanza as a statement, "We slowly drove," and an explanation—Death always gets where he's going without a rush, and his attentions meant that I was no longer in my former rush—then we can hear in the flow of the words and the bounce of the meter the way that the second statement clarifies the first. We should pause here to acknowledge that Dickinson's idiosyncratic punctuation makes our task a little longer. She prefers the dash to the colon, the semicolon, and the period. This poem even ends on a dash stop rather than a customary full stop. That makes my assertion that we should read from capital letter to period a bit harder, especially when she peppers in all those capitalized nouns all over the place. Even so, we can mostly tell when a statement is ending, even if the ending is approximate.

HERE'S A SLIGHTLY DIFFERENT ANGLE ON POETIC DICTION. THIS ONE, the beginning of "Kubla Khan," is by Samuel Taylor Coleridge (1772–1834), and describes, he says, "a Vision in a Dream":

> In Xanadu did Kubla Khan
> A stately pleasure dome decree:
> Where Alph, the sacred river, ran
> Through caverns measureless to man
>   Down to a sunless sea.

Read that aloud and listen for the tone. Do you hear the sense of grandeur in that opening? In fact, what do you hear? Strangeness, certainly. If you're like me the first time I read it, you have no idea about what either Xanadu or Alph might be, although you may have heard of Kublai Khan (or at least of that other Khan, Genghis). If we can characterize Dickinson's poem as narrative and conversational, this one is incantatory. Just that first line, with its exotic elements and the repetition of sounds ("-du did Ku-" along with the three *n* sounds and two *k*s), feels for all the world as if a spell is being cast. Which it is, make no mistake about that. The second line emphasizes that magical quality, "A stately pleasure dome decree." Now, it may be within the purview of a khan to decree a dome, but what is really magical are the sounds in the line, "pleasure" picking up the *l* in "stately" and the last two words alliterating (and picking up the *d* sounds from the first line) but then veering away from each other, along with the repeated *s* of "stately pleasure." That sibilance (which simply means the condition of having *s* sounds) will come at us furiously in the last two lines: "caverns measureless," "sunless sea." In fact, counting the *z* sound of "Xanadu," every line has at least one sibilant (hissing sound) in it. What we have, then, is a great deal of repetition of a comparative handful of sounds: *s* and *z*; *d* and its cousin, *t*; *m* and *n*; *l*; *k*; and the short *a* of "Xanadu" and "man." What also matters in terms of how the poem sounds is where those sounds occur. With the exception of "did" in line one, almost every key sound falls on a stressed syllable, "Ĭn Xánădú dĭd Kúblă Khán," and so on. While this emphasis tells us nothing about what the poem means nor even what we might do with that soundscape, it does begin to convey a feeling. When we find out later in the poem that the speaker is conveying a dream he had and we see that his language falls into a much more pedestrian profile when his retelling is interrupted and he loses the thread forever, we can look back on that opening and say, "Of course it would sound like that; this is the language of dream magic."

DID YOU CATCH THAT? IN DEALING WITH THE PATTERN OF STRESSED and unstressed syllables, called *scansion* (meaning where the stresses fall in lines of poetry), in the study of *prosody* (the broader study of technical matters involving meter and form), stressed syllables are indicated by an acute accent ("ác-cent"), while unstressed syllables are indicted by the tiny *u*, called a *breve*, over the syllable ("ac-cĕnt"; together, "ác-cĕnt" or "Xán-ă-dú"). Just one way of doing it. I tried ALL CAPS for stressed syllables, but it felt too much like shouting. And it's UG-ly.

Poems can also be discursive rather than narrative or pic-torial. Robert Frost frequently uses this strategy, nowhere to better effect than in "Birches" (1916):

> When I see birches bend to left and right
> Across the lines of straighter darker trees,
> I like to think some boy's been swinging them.
> But swinging doesn't bend them down
> As ice storms do.

Again, it is important to read this aloud in order to get the effect. In fact, read it several times in different ways. Or try to. Just try belting it out grandly as you can do with "Kubla Khan." For that matter, give it a shot as something to be chanted. Know what you'll find out? Not gonna happen. Just about the only way the poem can be read is the way Frost wants you to read it, as one person discussing something with another person. Indeed, this is an intensely personal poem, due to both subject matter and the way the words lead us to this conver-sational style. If you doubt, here's an experiment for you: write it out as sentences without line breaks or excess capital letters. You'll find yourself hard-pressed to tell that it was ever a poem. And yet—and here is a large part of his genius—the lines are completely regular met-rically: "Whĕn Í sĕe bírch-ĕs bénd tŏ léft ănd ríght ă-cróss thĕ línes ŏf stráight-ĕr dárk-ĕr trées, Ĭ líke tŏ thínk sŏme bóy's bĕen swíng-ĭng thém." Now, for heaven's sake, don't read it that way. But it remains true that this is the classic metrical form of English verse, *iambic pen-tameter.* That means that each line (excluding those where the poet varies the pattern) contains five metrical feet (the "penta-" part of the name), with each foot consisting of two syllables, an unstressed syllable followed by a stressed syllable—"da-DUM." There are plenty of other metrical arrangements, and we'll get to those later on, but one thing we can always count on with Frost is that he will employ one of those patterns. After all, he's the guy who said he'd no more write free verse (verse where there is no regular metrical pattern) than "play tennis with the net down."

This chapter is called "The Sounds of Sense," and so far we have been talking about how sense occurs in poetry. But sometimes the sounds of sense can be employed in the production of sheer nonsense:

> 'Twas brillig, and the slithy toves
>   Did gyre and gimble in the wabe:
> All mimsy were the borogoves,
>   And the mome raths outgrabe.
>
> "Beware the Jabberwock, my son!
>   The jaws that bite, the claws that catch!
> Beware the Jubjub bird, and shun
>   The frumious Bandersnatch!"

You will likely recognize this as the opening of Lewis Carroll's "Jabberwocky," a poem Alice discovers in *Through the Looking-Glass, and What Alice Found There* (1871). Compared to hers, your job is easy; Alice found the poem in the back-to-front world of the looking-glass and figured out it had to be held up to a mirror to be read left to right. Not so easy, is it? Be thankful for small favors.

What matters for our purposes is that hardly any of the content words (chiefly nouns and some verbs) mean anything in English. That's why Humpty Dumpty has to decode the thing for us afterwards. "Slithy," for instance, is a combination of "lithe" and "slimy," and he says, "It's like a portmanteau—there are two meanings packed up into one word." That is, in fact, where we get the notion of a portmanteau word, which is indispensable to those of us who are James Joyce

scholars—or like puns. You may know some words, such as the ne-
ologisms (newly created words) "galumphing" and "chortle," but you
would not have in 1871. All in all, this was and remains a very strange
reading experience. And yet . . . if we focus not on the content words
but on the function words—articles, conjunctions, and so on—this
is perfectly well-constructed English in a familiar poetic form. The
four-line stanza is iambic tetrameter (eight syllables with the stresses
on syllables 2, 4, 6, and 8) in the first three lines and a sometimes
irregular iambic trimeter (six syllables, emphasis on 2, 4, and 6) in
the fourth. Nothing too exotic there. We may have no idea what a
Jabberwock is, but we have no trouble with "Beware the Jabberwock,
my son!" In fact, it may make the alien words stranger to have a po-
etic form and language structure be so familiar. This formula serves
writers of *nonsense verse* (yes, it's a real thing) well from Carroll and
Edward Lear to John Lennon and Dr. Seuss. Because even nonsense
means something.

One aspect of most nonsense verse is that it is more regular, at
least in establishing a pattern initially, than "serious" verse. What
makes us able to read the nonsense is the regularity. Knowing where
words will appear and what part of speech they will likely be makes
it possible to predict the meaning of words that carry none. Con-
sider this couplet from Edward Lear's "The Owl and the Pussycat"
(also 1871, a very good year for silliness), "They dined on mince, and
slices of quince, / Which they ate with a runcible spoon." You all know
runcible spoons, right? No? Neither did Lear. It is a made-up word. He
didn't even intend for it to suggest any particular meaning. It has the
look of a word, in fact the look of an adjective (convenient, appearing
as it does in front of a noun), and it fills out two anapests: "with ă rún-
cĭ-blĕ spóon." The key to selling a counterfeit word is to make it fit in
as if it always belonged in the spot it occupies. In other words, watch
how Edward Lear does it.

Whether it's sense or nonsense poets seek, we do well to remem-
ber that sound is, in and of itself, a structural element in the construc-
tion of meaning. And sometimes just plain fun.

2

Sounds Beyond Sense

―――――――

SENTENCES MAKE SOUNDS. WHAT A CONCEPT! BUT POEMS ARE full of sounds and not all of them are meaningful. The sounds in a poem can prove useful beyond their work in creating meaning. Or rather, not all of them are present because of their contribution to meaning. The sounds that inhabit poems can become signature elements of poets' work. Seamus Heaney, for instance, loved the word "plash," which I'm guessing you have rarely had occasion to use. Or "plosive," another favorite. Heaney is so known for his love of strong consonants, especially those hard *g* and *k* sounds that come down to us from our Germanic linguistic ancestors, that the critic and professor Philip Hobsbaum said of one of his volumes that it was full of "the plop and gurgle of Heaneyspeak." He is one of a kind, but far from the only poet to consider sounds in their own right.

In order to get anywhere with this consideration of sound, we need a divorce. If this were a discussion of music, we could easily effect a separation between the melody and the lyrics. But when the source of the musicality is also the source of meaning, matters become trickier. The words contain the melody, the harmony, the counterpoint. So we have to push past words to their constituent sounds. If we blow the word "plash" apart, for instance, we have three items to work with: *pl*, a short *a* as in "hat," and *sh*, two consonant clusters and a vowel sound.

We need to get some concepts out of the way here. Consonants occur in pairs where one is said with a voice and one isn't. *P* and *b*, for instance, are both formed with bringing the lips together and then parting them with a puff of air.

Because to make the *b* sound you add a little voice to it, it is called, oddly enough, *voiced*. By contrast, *p* is voiceless. That means you can't say it with your voice, since that turns it into a *b* sound. Try it. Say "pay" and "bay" normally; then try saying "pay" while making sure to add your voice to the *p*. See what happens? To say "pay," you can't bring your voice in until after the *p*; if you do, you say "bay." As a result of this phenomenon—and you should feel phenomenal just about now—a word beginning with *p* is always going to sound more, well, plosive than one starting with *b*.

Consonants, by the way, are classified as *plosives, fricatives, liquids*, and words like *glottal* and *bilabial*, to say nothing of *alveopalatal* and *interdental*, sneak in. We'll try to avoid them as much as possible. When linguists talk shop, about half the time it sounds like some sort of pornographic code. And that wouldn't do, would it?

Add to that plosive *p* the *liquid* (meaning the way *l* and *r* are formed in the mouth) of the *l* right after *p* and then the short *a* in the middle and that sibilant *sh* at the end, and you have a word that sounds like what it means, beginning with a hard bounce on the diving board and ending with a ripped entry into the water. What's not to love? Plash, indeed.

Boggled yet? Sorry about that. What we're saying is that we can break words down into their sounds, and at that level, as with quantum physics, things get a little strange. But once you know how letters and their possible sounds work, you can have all kinds of fun. Poets string similar sounds together all the time. If they happen at the beginning of words, as in "string similar sounds," we call that *alliteration*. If they are sprinkled through a passage but not necessarily next door to one another or even in the same place in the words, we call that *consonance* (if they're consonants, naturally) or *assonance* (if they're vowels, less naturally but just go with it). If they're happening at the ends of words in large enough groups, we speak of *rhyme*, which is the one you already know for sure. Rhyme requires critical mass: the mere presence of *s* at the ends of words does not constitute rhyme, nor even "-ers," but words ending in "-thers" as in "fathers" and "mothers" just might work even if the first syllables don't align.

Let's spend a moment here to give body to these abstractions:

- **Alliteration**—a series of words in succession (or near succession) all beginning with the same sound, as in Shakespeare's Sonnet 30, which begins, "When to the sessions of sweet silent thought." It doesn't matter right now whether we understand this or not; the repeated initial *s* sounds in "sessions of sweet silent" create a soundscape to begin the poem. That sibilance is enhanced by the second *s* in "sessions" and, I've always suspected, the *th* of "thought." That's a mighty soft sound palette, but for our term, only the initial sounds matter.

- **Consonance**—a series of words in close proximity employing the same or related sounds. The more familiar alliteration is a special instance of consonance in which the repeated sounds appear at the beginning of words. More generally, however, consonant repetition can appear anywhere in the words. The final two lines of Emily Dickinson's "'Twas later when the summer went" demonstrate consonance using both *t* and *th* sounds: "Yet *th*a*t* pa*th*e*t*ic pendulum / Keeps esoteric time." That's five instances of *t* in two short lines, plus two uses of *th* and one *d*, which acts as a sort of bridge between the two, being the voiced partner to the unvoiced *t*. And we can throw in three uses of the hard *c/k* in "pathetic / Keeps esoteric"—virtually every word here is adding to the soundscape of the lines. Note that, unlike alliteration, these sounds occur at various points in words. The poem as a whole (only eight lines) is often cited for its consonance using *m* and *n* sounds, and while these two lines maintain that pattern, they establish one of their own.

- **Assonance**—a series of uses of the same vowel sound in close proximity. Using the same Dickinson poem, we can note that the short *e* sound appears in "Y*e*t," "path*e*tic," "p*e*ndulum," and "*e*soteric." We can debate whether that sound is compromised in the last instance by the *r* that follows it, but I think that counts.

What does all this mean for poetry readers? Chiefly that we spend a good deal of time tracing patterns not of words but of letters and their associated sounds. Or sometimes we don't because we're bludgeoned by it. Gerard Manley Hopkins (1844–89), one of the strangest poets ever to write in English, has a line in his poem "The Windhover" that's a real showstopper, "shéer plód makes plough down sillion shine." Don't know what it means? Neither does anyone else, and I have some doubts about Hopkins himself. First of all, you'd have to know that "sillion" is an archaism for "furrow," and no student has ever known that. Ever. And then he leaves off the ending of "plodding," which knocks us for a loop, and loses a possible "the" before "plough" and "sillion," each of which would be a nice touch. If we restore those, the meaning is something like "the drudgery of the plow going through the furrow keeps it shiny" (remember, this was in an age before tractors and plowing behind a horse or mule was the very essence of plodding). But who cares? The line is a blast to say out loud. Why is that? It's the way that Hopkins stacks up familial sounds. *S* and *sh* appear four times, "*sh*éer plód make*s* plough down *s*illion *sh*ine," *p* twice, *r* and *l* combined four times. And then there are the vowels. The *o* in "pl*o*d" morphs into a long *ou* in "pl*ou*gh" and "d*ow*n" before changing again into a short *yo* in "sill*io*n." The long *e* of "sheer" chimes, if only slightly, with the short *i* of "s*i*llion" and then lengthens into "sh*i*ne." And it's a sonnet, so there are thirteen more lines that are just as wacky, which is why he's one of my favorite poets. And, as you might suppose, of our plashing friend, the young Heaney.

Right there, I think, is the basic tension of poetry: *Meaning lies in words, melody in sounds.* The trick lies in bringing them together. Too little emphasis on sounds, you've got prose, and not necessarily very interesting prose. Too little emphasis on words, you can wind up with gibberish. Lovely gibberish, perhaps, but nonsense nonetheless. But aren't words made of sounds? you ask. And therefore sounds only exist in words? Yes, but that doesn't mean they inevitably play nicely together. Stay tuned.

REMEMBER "PLASH"? IT LEADS US TO ANOTHER ELEMENT OF WORDS as sounds: onomatopoeia, or words that sound like the things they describe. Sometimes they are single words, sometimes whole passages, even whole poems, as in Edgar Allan Poe's "The Bells":

> *Hear the sledges with the bells—*
> *Silver bells!*
> *What a world of merriment their melody foretells!*
> *How they tinkle, tinkle, tinkle,*
> *In the icy air of night!*
> *While the stars that oversprinkle*
> *All the heavens, seem to twinkle*
> *With a crystalline delight;*
> *Keeping time, time, time,*
> *In a sort of Runic rhyme,*
> *To the tintinnabulation that so musically wells*
> *From the bells, bells, bells, bells,*
> *Bells, bells, bells—*
> *From the jingling and the tinkling of the bells.*
> (1849)

The first part will be plenty for our purposes here. Gee, do you think Poe wants us to hear bells? It isn't just the word "bells" repeated over and over and over again. And over some more. It's also the "jingling" and "tinkling" that's going on, along with all of the *l* sounds throughout the passage from "sledges" to "silver" to "crystalline" to "musically," not to mention the several words that rhyme with "bells." And in their midst that percussive "tintinnabulation," sounding like a series of clapper strikes. Later in the poem, the sounds that go with the bells won't be so bright, as in the final movement when we hear funereal bells "moan." Here, though, all is air and light. The poem is exemplary. Depending on your point of view, this is either a great example of onomatopoeia or a cautionary warning that such things can be taken too far. Regardless of how we may see the outcome, we have to accept that there are few poems so thoroughgoing in seeking to embody the sounds they describe.

How about another poem with bells but maybe less bombast? In "anyone lived in a pretty how town"—and yes, that is worded accurately—E. E. Cummings has this line: "(with up so floating many bells down)." Twice. We will investigate the Case of the Fractured Word Order elsewhere. For the moment, however, I only want you to hear what that line says about the sound of bells. Consider how, first, the peal of a bell seems to float out on the air before it dissipates in what we may hear as a soft landing back on earth. As we read the poem aloud, we register the participial "floating" as a lighter, less concluded sound than "float" or "floats." In fact, we may well hear—I do—the line as two halves, the airier "with up so floating" taking us to a turning point where "many bells down" not only carries us earthward in meaning but also ends on the heavier final sound in "down." He further accentuates the sounds of bells through self-rhymes ("all by all and deep by deep") as well as straightforward onomatopoeia ("women and men(both dong and ding)") and rather thoroughgoing sound repetitions throughout the poem. Less blustering than Poe's belfry, perhaps, but memorable nonetheless.

PILING UP SOUNDS

IN *THE SOUNDS of Poetry*, Robert Pinsky introduces the terms "consonant-thread" and "vowel-thread" for the scarier "consonance" and "assonance." This is probably a useful switch, being more descriptive, especially since few things can bring the young at heart to giggles quicker than "assonance," particularly as you write it on the board. What he is talking about, however, is absolutely central to the poetic project: How does a particular poem stack up vowel or consonant sounds, and what is the effect of that stacking?

One possible effect might be, for some readers, too much. I am rather a fan of too-muchness, but that position is not universal. Here would be Exhibit A, the octave (first eight lines) of that Hopkins sonnet, "The Windhover":

> *I caught this morning morning's minion, king-*
> > *dom of daylight's dauphin, dapple-dawn-drawn Falcon,*
> > > *in his riding*
> > *Of the rolling level underneath him steady air, and striding*
> *High there, how he rung upon the rein of a wimpling wing*
> *In his ecstasy! then off, off forth on swing,*
> > *As a skate's heel sweeps smooth on a bow-bend: the hurl*
> > > *and gliding*
> > *Rebuffed the big wind. My heart in hiding*
> *Stirred for a bird, – the achieve of, the mastery of the thing!*

Whew! Try that one out loud. Actually, it is one of my favorites to read aloud, partly because the opportunities to crash and burn are so numerous, and partly because, as day-two fodder in my British modernism course, it made everything after it seem pretty tame.

THAT'S MORE ALLITERATION THAN MOST POETS WOULD BE WILLING to undertake. Really—split "kingdom" at the end of line one because a mere five words starting with *d* in line two was insufficient? To see consonance (or consonant-threading) at work, look at the following line, with all the liquid sounds, "Of the *rolling level* under*neath* him steady ai*r*, and st*r*iding / High the*r*e," appearing in initial, middle, and terminal positions in words. And indeed, it carries over to line four, where the *r* sounds shift to *w* sounds in "wimpling wing." It's actually hard to read without sounding like Elmer Fudd. So dominant are those liquid sounds in the two lines that we might not notice the frequency of nasal consonants (*m* and *n*, so called because there's a push of air from the nostrils when saying them). That would be unfortunate; by my count, there are ten of them there. One more audacious thing about those eight lines: the rhyme scheme—the pattern of rhymed lines, which we usually indicate by an individual letter for each sound—is A. Okay, AAAAAAAA. Who does that? Hopkins, that's who. It is actually a great relief when the sestet (the final six lines) rhyme BCBCBC. Variety is good.

You can read pretty much the rest of poetry in English and not find anyone like Hopkins. He bases his personal poetics on a very old Welsh practice called *cynghanedd*, a system of stress, alliteration, repetition, and rhyme. The rules are too complex to go into here, but they fit in with Hopkins's own tendencies to wreak havoc on normal meter with what he called *sprung rhythm*, in which he moves stresses (by means of capitalization, boldface, and exclamation marks) onto syllables or words not normally stressed to get idiosyncratic effects. And they are idiosyncratic all right. But what's the point of using the sounds letters can make if not to wring all the music possible from them?

What the Heck Is It?

IT WOULD SEEM REASONABLE THAT IF WE WANT TO TALK about reading a literary form, we should define the object of study, don't you think? After all, how hard can it be? Poems have been around for thousands of years in one form or another. And virtually everyone who has ever written (or seemingly read) a poem has had a go at defining it.

So just tell us what a poem is already.

You know, we're not going to get anywhere if you insist on being rational. True enough, lots of folks have told us what a poem is. Generally, they've left us none the wiser. Here are some candidates for the Hall of Fame in the Unhelpful Definition category:

- Robert Frost: "[A poem is] a momentary stay against confusion." "Poetry is what gets lost in translation."
- Thomas Hardy: "Poetry is emotion put into measure."
- Percy Bysshe Shelley: "Poetry is the record of the best and happiest moments of the happiest and best minds."
- Samuel Taylor Coleridge: "Poetry: the best words in the best order."

- Marianne Moore: "Poetry is the art of creating imaginary gardens with real toads."
- Christopher Fry: "Poetry is the language in which man explores his own amazement."

And these are giants of the form! So you tell me, if you took these collectively, could you tell me what a poem *is*? I've cheated, of course. These great poets are trying mostly to speak about *poetry*, not *a poem*; as such they're more invested mythologizing their art than in producing workable definitions for the student. Clearly, if we're going to come up with anything, we're going to have to do it ourselves. So what do you think a poem is, class? And bear in mind, I have heard every one of these from students.

- *It's made of words?* As are many things. So then, true, if not entirely helpful.
- *It's written in lines?* Except when it's not. Again, some truth in there.
- *It rhymes.* Again, except when it doesn't and in some eras but not others.
- *What about rhythm?* Yes, what about it? Frequently true. Then again . . .
- *It follows its own rules.* Now you might be getting somewhere.
- *The language is colorful, flowery, and sometimes hard to understand.* There's a little number about a red wheelbarrow that I'd like to show you.

Poems are easier to talk about than to define. The difficulty isn't so much the observable features (lines with definite breaks, rhythm and meter, special forms and rules, a bent for figurative language) as the exceptions. There is virtually no aspect of poetry we can delineate for which exceptions don't instantly raise their ugly heads. On the one hand, there is the sonnet, fourteen gorgeous lines about which virtually all of your observations nearly always apply. On the other, there's the prose poem, which may share with other poetry (or a lot of it) only the aspect of brevity—so brief, in fact, that it can't even qualify as short-short story or "flash fiction." Or maybe that other hand is a poem by E. E. Cummings that is a full page tall with no line over three letters. Yes, *letters*, not words. You see what we're up against?

But let's go back to those various definitions from the famous and notorious. What, if anything, do they have in common? Let me stipulate here that our gathered giants, aside from Fry, who wrote verse dramas, are all practitioners within the *lyric*, rather than the *narrative*, tradition of poetry. Narrative poems are those that tell a story, whereas when we speak of lyric poetry, we mean those poems that are relatively short, somewhat compressed, and often a little musical. Not for nothing do we speak of a song's lyrics: "lyric" comes from "lyre," the stringed instrument used to accompany such po-ems in ancient Greece. If you're like most folks, nearly every poem you've ever read falls into this category.

So then, let's look at the commonalities among the state-ments: They are telling us that, first of all, poetry often (if not always) seeks to explore our deepest thoughts, feelings, and experiences. Second, many of the statements speak to the *compression* of poetry. Lyric poems especially say much in small spaces. If you have ever read Homer's *The Iliad* or John Milton's *Paradise Lost*, you may quite properly have doubts about the compressed nature of poetry. That combination of depth and compression creates an *intensity* that is the hall-mark of the lyric poem. Third, poetry helps us look at the world in a new way. It shakes us out of our usual complacency and offers us a new perspective. After all, who among us ever thought about a fork in the road before Robert Frost made us really see its significance in "The Road Not Taken"? That's what Marianne Moore is talking about when she speaks of "imaginary gardens with real toads in them."

Poems can surprise, ambush, astonish, and delight or dismay us. And that is the final common element of those statements from the masters: implicit in their pronouncements is that poetry gives pleasure. That pleasure may be aesthetic, linguistic, emotional, intellectual, or visceral. It can take a thousand different forms. The formal delight that we may take from an E. E. Cummings poem will be different from the intellectual rewards of T. S. Eliot's "The Love Song of J. Alfred Prufrock" or the emotional fulfillment of Walt Whitman's *Song of Myself*, yet their variety reminds us of the larger truth: whatever the form, the poem will be aimed at giving readers some sort of pleasure. We can be certain that very few poets have ever sat down to a clean sheet of paper or empty computer screen and said to themselves, Let's see about writing something that readers are going to find profoundly unpleasant. Not saying it has never happened, only that it is rare.

POETRY LAB

You know what's really wrong with those definitions? Nothing. I like them all. The problem, for the most part, isn't that they are untrue but that they are true for the poet writing them. Thomas Hardy could scarcely make a truer statement than "Poetry is emotion put into measure." For *his* poetry. Or take Shelley, the poet of ecstatic experience, saying that it is a record of the best and happiest thoughts of the happiest and best minds. Read his "To a Skylark" and you'll see that it fits him like a tailored suit. But they don't necessarily prove helpful with poetry in general.

Having trashed numerous members of the verse pantheon, it is only fair that I offer my own inadequate stab at defining poetry, so here goes. **A poem is an experiment with and in language, an attempt to discover how best to capture its subject and make readers see it anew.** In so doing, the poem makes its exploration of language part of the subject, becoming both the experiment and the laboratory where it takes place.

This is not inevitably true of prose. Dubious? Then consider: novels of a certain sort are often praised by being called "poetic"; poems are almost never praised by being called "novelistic." And "prosaic" is a term of derogation.

I will freely admit that my definition lacks that truth-and-beauty clarion call of the more high-flown descriptions. If, however, we understand the writing of a poem as a sort of exploration where the artifact produced is both the record of that exploration and the act of exploring, then we begin to understand that writing a poem is a struggle with, in, and through language.

Remember, as Stéphane Mallarmé puts it, poems are made not out of ideas but out of words. And words have a nasty habit of refusing to go where we send them, or declining to carry the weight that we put upon them. The poet, then, must get these churlish demons to stay where she puts them and ultimately do her bidding. She must arrange them in a way that accounts for not only semantic needs but also auditory and visual considerations—who cares what you have to say if your saying it is ugly or inept?—while avoiding unwanted secondary meanings and unintended double entendres. It's a little like crossing a field where every step is guaranteed to encounter either a land mine or a pitfall: Do you prefer getting blown up or falling to your demise? And still, people keep wanting the job. Simply astonishing.

The experiment is always new, always beginning again. Whatever worked in the last poem offers no assurance that the same strategy will work this time. Of course, a great many poets have tried to make repeat performances work, hence the disappointment that so often creeps into our reading. The poets who excite us, who continually court danger, are those who take up each new challenge as a double-dog dare to be fresh.

Now, within that freshness, there are limitations. It can be nearly impossible to write out of one's own time. No one today can write like an eighteenth-century poet, any more than those poets could have written poems in the manner of our contemporaries. There are limits, after all, to freshness and novelty. What, then, should we make of poetic practice? That it is beholden to its cultural moment, replete with that moment's philosophical, intellectual, social, and aesthetic trends. That it moves incrementally in most eras, and that extreme shifts happen infrequently. After the Romantic revolution, circa 1800, English poetry calmed down for a hundred years or so, until Modernism upended numerous Victorian applecarts. That it struggles constantly against the forces—societal, personal, even artistic—that would pull it toward the average. That it never wants to be merely average.

How
Is
Poetry?

3

Redeeming the Time

W HAT'S THAT? YOU DON'T UNDERSTAND THIS WHOLE "METER"
thing? As far as you can tell, Iambic's last name is Pentameter?
And you think rhythm should be followed by blues? Welcome to the
club. There is perhaps nothing about poetry that is as disconcerting as
the whole business of meter and rhythm. What about all those terrible
things we call lines of poetry in English? You know, trochaic trime-
ter and dactylic hexameter, that sort of nonsense. Another linguistic
accident: an unholy marriage of Greek terminology filtered through
Latin. That sort of thing begets monsters. But it is the terminology, not
the lines, that are monstrous. Here's the basic fact: for most of its his-
tory, poetry in English has been built on a foundation of lines that in
turn are built out of words arranged to form rhythmic patterns. These
patterns can—and often do—find their way into songs. And once we
know the basic patterns, we have only to count how often they repeat
in a line to name it.

Forget Greek; think music. With a little arithmetic. **Find the
beat, then count it off.**

Let's move a little slowly here; this stuff can make heads spin.
First, the one word you might know: "iamb." Which, for the record,
isn't one; it's a trochee (more in a moment). An iamb is a metrical *foot*

(which means a repeatable pattern of stresses) composed of an un-stressed syllable followed by a stressed syllable, which we can denote as "da-DUM" (as in "weak-STRONG"). "Succeed" is an iamb. So is "elect." Its paired opposition, metrically, is "trochee," which unlike "iamb" is the thing it designates, a pair of syllables in which the first is stressed—"DUM-da," or, in this case, "TRO-chee." Or "I-amb."

Here's the thing to remember: the metrical foot is independent of the word. That is to say, sometimes the poetic line may use "suc-ceed" as a complete metrical foot, in this case an iamb, but it is just as likely to split it, so that "suc-" is the second syllable of a trochee, while "-CEED" is the first syllable in another one. In that particular line, the poet might have options to use "FLOUR-ish" or "TRI-umph," but the meter dictates a word with the second syllable accented, so "suc-CEED" would be the choice. Is it any surprise that we get confused about all of this? Try to remember this: **In metrical counting, words don't matter; syllables do.**

METER AT WORK

LET'S PUT THIS newfound knowledge into practice. Here is the open-ing quatrain of a fairly famous poem. Good news here—there's not one word in it that you don't know, and only one funky ending:

> That time of year thou may'st in me behold
> When yellow leaves, or none, or few, do hang
> Upon those boughs which shake against the cold,
> Bare ruin'd choirs, where late the sweet birds sang.

Even if you don't know about the poet, you know that the poem is old, right? Not a lot of poets in the twentieth and twenty-first centuries have gone around using "thou" or "may'st," although the number isn't quite zero. This sonnet has a number, 73, and it belongs to Shakespeare, which puts it back a spell (the original book of his sonnets appeared in 1609). We'll come back to it as a poetic statement later on, but for now we're just talking about rhythm and meter. And the meter here is iambic pentameter, or five of those little "da-DUM" iambs laid end to end to make a line: "Thăt tíme ŏf yéar thŏu máy'st ĭn mé bĕ-hóld," with syllables 2, 4, 6, 8, and 10 stressed. Same thing in the next two lines—stresses on the even syllables. But then something different in line four: "Báre rúin'd chóirs, whĕre láte thĕ swéet bĭrds sáng." Whoa! That's not iambic or pentameter. Two things stand out here. First, we have that hammering effect of three consecutive stressed syllables, after which we can hardly find our bearings to see if any iambs remain (they do). And after we get over that rhythmic shock, we discover that somebody stole a syllable; it's tough to have five iambs with only nine syllables. So we have only nine, but six of those are stressed. Is that even legal? Yes, it is. **Meter isn't law; it's framework.** If it is slavishly followed as law, moreover, the result is monotonous and more often than not unintentionally funny. We actually need relief from the pattern every once in a while, at least where lyric poetry is concerned.

NARRATIVE POEMS ARE ANOTHER STORY. THIS ONE HAS A DIFFERENT pattern at work. True, it has a few squirrelly words, but they're either made up or borrowed from Native American lore, and in any case, they don't get in the way of the meaning:

> *By the shore of Gitche Gumee,*
> *By the shining Big-Sea-Water,*
> *At the doorway of his wigwam,*
> *In the pleasant Summer morning,*
> *Hiawatha stood and waited.*
> *All the air was full of freshness,*
> *All the earth was bright and joyous,*
> *And before him, through the sunshine,*
> *Westward toward the neighboring forest*
> *Passed in golden swarms the Ahmo,*

Passed the bees, the honey-makers,
Burning, singing in the sunshine.

This is music of a different sort. And compared to Shakespeare, practically brand-new. Henry Wadsworth Longfellow, in 1855, produced one of the great American epics, *The Song of Hiawatha*, of which this is the beginning of the final chapter, "Hiawatha's Departure."

The first thing you will notice, especially if you've just read Shakespeare's sonnet opening, is that somebody moved the stresses. They are in front of their unstressed partners, giving us "DUM-da, DUM-da." Or maybe you notice that the lines are shorter; you see that change even before reading it. Don't discount cues like this, which tell us simply by taking up less of the page that the count of metrical feet will be smaller. Here, there are four feet per line. We call that one *tetrameter*, meaning "four feet" (think of it as four bounces, "UP-down"). And the feet themselves? Trochees. Put them together and you get *trochaic tetrameter*, or "trochees times four." So why this particular arrangement of stresses for this long poem? For one thing, there's a touch of cultural appropriation here: Longfellow is aiming for a drumbeat pattern. And as we know from our classic Western movies, drumbeats never arrange themselves into iambs.

On top of that, the comparatively short lines and symmetry (four feet split evenly in a way that five feet never do) encourages readers to march along, line after line for a very long time, four beats and forward, four beats and forward. For Longfellow in this poem, the goal is to drive us down the page and over to the next page and the next and the next. Which is important because there are a lot of next pages.

The third of these elements is what's called the "feminine" ending. All that means is that the last syllable of the line is unstressed. Stressed final syllables are called "masculine." We will just have to get past the inherent sexism—strength is manly, and so on—and agree that neither you nor I chose the names. While I don't find unstressed syllables particularly gendered one way or another, I do find them slightly unfinished when they end a line. I suppose my ear is attuned to the cadences of iambs and lines ending on the beat. We can return to the matter of line endings and sex another time, but this discussion is enough trauma for now.

So there you have it. Two poems, two different meters with stresses reversed and line lengths varied. There are lots more options where those came from. One of these is pentameter, the other tetrameter. So just how many meters are there? There is theoretically no limit, although practically the number is small. Thank goodness! One can hardly imagine a single-foot line: just two syllables, and then on to the next line of just two, and so on, marching the metrical order down the page. A two-foot line is slightly more likely, which is why there is actually a word for it, "dimeter," although I have yet to see one that doesn't take frequent liberties with both meter and number of syllables. Here are the usual suspects:

- **Dimeter:** two metrical feet (of whatever shape, as with all of these)
- **Trimeter:** three metrical feet
- **Tetrameter:** four
- **Pentameter:** five
- **Hexameter:** six
- **Heptameter:** seven
- **Octameter:** eight
- *Beyond here there be monsters . . .*

This isn't so tough. If we ignore the "meters," we recognize those prefixes from "di-" (as in "dichotomy") to "tri-" (as in pretty much everything) and "penta-" (as in the Pentagon) to "hepta-" (as in the once every four years the heptathlon women's track multievent). True, "tetra-"doesn't come up much in everyday speech, so that one you may have to commit to memory; the rest, however, you can mostly figure out. Better still, the shortest one and the longest two don't occur very often in nature, so we really only have recourse to trimeter, tetrameter, pentameter, and hexameter on a regular basis.

So that's how lines count off their feet, but how do we reckon the feet themselves? Because there are names, although, alas, they are all Greek. And their number for our purposes is five:

- **Iamb:** an unstressed syllable followed by a stressed syllable—"da-DUM," as in "de-LAY" or, pronounced correctly, "de-TROIT"
- **Trochee:** the opposite, a stressed followed by an unstressed syllable—"DUM-da," as in "THOM-as FOS-ter"
- **Spondee:** two stressed syllables in a row—"DUM-DUM," as in "DUMB-DUMB"
- **Anapest:** a three-syllable foot, two unstressed syllables followed by one stressed—"da-da-DUM," as in "in the HOUSE"
- **Dactyl:** the reverse, one stressed syllable followed by two unstressed ones: "DUM-da-da," as in "NOT a chance"
- There are others, but do you really need to know that "pyrrhic" is the term for two unaccented syllables hanging out together, or that there are words for three unaccented syllables or three accented syllables that form a poetic foot? Thought not.

Those are the five terms we need to discuss virtually all situations that will arise in English metrical verse. And as with line lengths, we can dispense with a couple of these. For obvious reasons, spondees hardly ever flock together. Think about it: a line of spondaic pentameter would be *ten consecutive stressed syllables*. Likely? Not very. Dactyls, for their part, are great ways to start lines, less great as ways to end them (those two unstressed syllables feel like something fizzling out). As a result, we often see them used in concert with other feet, as with Walt Whitman's "Óut ŏf thĕ crá-dlĕ énd-lĕss-lĭ róck-ĭng," which alternates a dactyl with a trochee, repeated. The term for such mixing within a line is *logaoedic*, but I recommend you forget it and remember the concept. Now, being Whitman, he doesn't maintain the pattern throughout but reverts to free verse, although he does begin many key lines with a dactyl, which imparts a sort of forward momentum.

Anapests appear more frequently as the organizing foot of poems, but they appear more frequently in comic verse than in serious poetry, favored by such bards of merriment as Lewis Carroll and Dr. Seuss. The example you know best, in all likelihood, comes around every year:

> 'Twas the NIGHT be-fore CHRIST-mas and ALL
> through the HOUSE
> Not a CREA-ture was STIR-ring, not E-ven a MOUSE.

Sort of makes you have more respect, doesn't it? And the fact that it is also the meter of *The Cat in the Hat*, although Dr. Seuss breaks those longer lines of Clement Clarke Moore's in half and makes two lines of each one. Young readers, short lines, you understand.

And trochees? I've already given you the chief example of trochaic verse in *The Song of Hiawatha*. Those lines are *trochaic tetrameter* (trochee times four): "Bý thĕ shóre ŏf Gít-chĕ Gú-mĕe, / Bý thĕ shín-ĭng Bíg-Sĕa-Wá-tĕr," giving Longfellow the drumbeat sort of rhythm

What we're talking about here is *scansion*, the analysis of how metrical arrangements play out in the real world, or how a line *scans*. We should remember that meter is merely the framework over which a poem is stretched. When we examine the actual poem, we not only find out what the baseline meter is but also how and where (and maybe why) the poem departs from that pattern. And what we're really doing is finding out why we feel what we feel about the poem's rhythm. The names of things don't matter so much as that we can see what's going on metrically; the names just make it possible for us to discuss what we're seeing. Neither of us will likely remember that those three stressed words, "Bare ruin'd choirs," have a name (*molossus*). Or care.

As you have intuited, metrical feet and line length inevitably get together. Knowing that a verse is written in pentameter tells us nothing until we know what sort of foot is repeated five times over. Among other things, a dactylic pentameter line would be longer than its iambic cousin by five syllables, a not inconsiderable number. At the same time, the iambic line will end on a stress, while the stressed syllable of the last dactyl has to look over two unstressed colleagues to see the end of the line. All of which is to say that they have little in common except a fivefold pattern.

METRICAL OPTIONS

I suggested earlier that metrical lines over six beats (roughly twelve syllables) are uncommon. That, however, doesn't mean they don't exist. Consider this bit of iambic octameter (eight feet of whatever meter) silliness from W. S. Gilbert's *The Pirates of Penzance*:

> *I am the very model of a modern Major-General,*
> *I've information vegetable, animal, and mineral,*
> *I know the kings of England, and I quote the fights historical*
> *From Marathon to Waterloo, in order categorical;*
> *I'm very well-acquainted, too, with matters mathematical,*
> *I understand equations, both the simple and quadratical,*
> *About binomial theorem I'm teeming with a lot o' news,*
> *With many cheerful facts about the square of the hypote-*
> > *nuse.*

Now, for best results, it needs to be spoken (or sung, if you know the tune) very fast. That's in the nature of what are called *patter songs*, in which Gilbert and Sullivan specialized in their comic operas. One thing that you might notice here is the inversion of nouns and adjectives at the ends of lines. Taking this sort of liberty is often referred to as *poetic license*, or one aspect of it, by which we mean the freedom we accord poets to abuse certain conventions of grammar or word order to achieve desired effects. The desired effect here, beyond metrical arrangement and rhyme scheme, is comedy. "Order categorical" is just funny, to say nothing of "I understand equations, both the simple and quadratical." Very long lines are frequently employed, to the extent that anything about them is frequent, for either comic or gothic effects. Some will disagree with my declaration of the meter here, and indeed other scansion arrangements can be argued. But if we hear both strong and weak stresses here (GÉN-ĕr-ál), the eight stresses appear more clearly.

If we turn the beat around and go looking for trochaic, rather than iambic, rhythm, we find Edgar Allan Poe and something decidedly not comic:

> *Once upon a midnight dreary, while I pondered, weak*
> *   and weary,*
> *Over many a quaint and curious volume of forgotten*
> *   lore—*
> *   While I nodded, nearly napping, suddenly there came*
> *   a tapping,*
> *As of some one gently rapping, rapping at my chamber*
> *   door.*

Poe dips deep into his bag of tricks to invoke a dark and foreboding atmosphere. Trochees in and of themselves are not spooky—once you get to know them—but he also employs *internal rhyme* (rhymes within lines themselves, as in "dreary"/"weary" in line one and "napping"/"tapping"/"rapping" in lines three and four), and words of a certain heaviness ("pondered," "weary," "nodded," "curious"). The passage is a few ounces away from being leaden, but those ounces make all the difference.

NOW, HAVING LAID OUT THE POSSIBILITIES FOR HOW MANY METRICAL feet might appear in a line, we have to get confusing. You might think that a stanza would be made up of lines that are all the same length. That would be logical. It would also be wrong. Line length can vary within stanzas so long as the variation is consistent and therefore predictable. If you write a stanza in which the lines contain four, three, two, five, six, and four feet, nobody's going to want to sit with you at lunch, especially if the next one has a completely different pattern. Hey, it's a tough crowd in the poets' cafeteria. If, on the other hand, you alternate, say, four metrical feet in lines one and three and three metrical feet in lines two and four, it's all good. In fact, that is a famous arrangement called *common meter* (*ballad meter*) or *common measure* (*ballad measure*), fabled in story and song. Particularly song. You've been hearing it all your life:

> Ĭt ráined ăll níght thĕ dáy Ĭ léft,
> thĕ wéa-thĕr ít wăs drý,
> thĕ sún sŏ hót Ĭ fróze tŏ déath,
> Sŭ-sán-nă dón't yoŭ crý.

Maybe "Oh, Susanna" isn't as much of a hit in elementary schools as it was years ago, but I seem to recall singing it every year in music class. Okay, if that isn't seared into your brain, maybe this is:

> Ă-máz-ĭng gráce, hŏw swéet thĕ sóund
> thăt sáved ă wrétch lĭke mé!
> Ĭ ónce wăs lóst bŭt nów ăm fóund,
> wăs blínd bŭt nów Ĭ sée.

or,

> Ŏh, béau-tĭ-fúl, fŏr spá-cioŭs skíes,
> fŏr ám-bĕr wáves ŏf gráin,
> fŏr púr-plĕ móun-tăins' máj-ĕs-tý
> ă-bóve thĕ frúit-ĕd pláin.

We begin to see the pattern here, if we get past the really ugly orthography: 4–3–4–3 line alternation with rhymes on the second and fourth lines. "Amazing Grace" is the odd song out, with its rhyming of the odd-numbered lines as well. Oh, and always with iambs. If it isn't iambic, I think, the measure isn't all that common. As regards rhyme scheme, sometimes the two lines are written out as one, as in "The Yellow Rose of Texas": "She's the yellow rose of Texas, that I am going to see / Nobody else could miss her, not half as much as me." Those lines are often called *fourteeners*, because they contain fourteen syllables. This, of course, has nothing to do with meter and everything about how the eye perceives the page. The mere appearance of fourteen-syllable lines makes us uneasy, even if we're used to prose filling much more of the available space. On the other hand, we see the lines as published and instantly think, I can get through that.

As you might expect, the common measure is not unknown to poets who are not writing words for music. This is from the final section of Samuel Taylor Coleridge's "The Rime of the Ancient Mariner":

> Făre-wéll, făre-wéll! bŭt thís Ĭ téll
> tŏ thée, thŏu wéd-dĭng guést!
> Hĕ práy-ĕth wéll, whŏ lóv-ĕth wéll
> bŏth mán ănd bírd ănd béast.

> Hĕ práy-ĕth bést, whŏ lóv-ĕth bést
> áll thĭngs gréat ănd smáll;
> fŏr thĕ déar Gód whŏ lóv-ĕth ús,
> Hĕ máde ănd lóv-ĕth áll.

As with pretty much everything he does, Coleridge takes liberties with the common measure. You'll notice here that he, too, rhymes the odd-numbered lines, which is not standard. He also sometimes has stanzas that have six lines—still following the odd-even pattern—and in at least one case doubles the odd line, so that his pattern is 4–3–4–4–3, but just for that one stanza. If you're a genius, you can take liberties.

One of the attractions of common measure is that it works for ballads, which can be long. It can be carried along with or without melody for many stanzas—"The Ancient Mariner" finishes up at 625 lines (the odd number reflecting that one eccentric stanza). We can follow along in part because the rhythm drives us to the next line and the next stanza. It becomes a sort of rhythmic engine to carry the poem forward. But even poets who write very short poems can fall in love with common measure, as Dickinson proves in poem after poem, which is why the vast majority of her poems can be sung to the tune of "The Yellow Rose of Texas." Sure, you can do it to "America the Beautiful," but it won't be as much fun.

And that brings us to a critical observation: having learned to find the stresses, *IGNORE THEM*. Read poems as naturally as you can. Stresses will make themselves known without any outside assistance. Every poem has its own rhythm and its own melody. Don't bang the drum. Listen for the music.

4

The Rhythm(s) of the Saints

FEEL A LITTLE BEATEN UP? I MEAN, SERIOUSLY, "METER," "IAMB," "anapest," "meter," "trochee," "meter," blah, blah, blah. For a whole chapter, no less! On the one hand, I feel I should apologize for going all technical here. Why does all that meter business matter? If you are a poet who might wish to write, say, a sonnet, that knowledge is critical. We regular readers, by contrast, will likely never have that level of intimacy with the demands and rewards of meter. Instead, we need language instruction. Every art form has its own language, its own special way of communicating, with a complete set of rules and practices amounting to a grammar. We're not talking English here, but the particulars of poem construction. "Iamb," for instance, isn't simply a term to bedevil us from the start, although it may have that effect, but a tool to be used by the poet and therefore understood by the reader. After all, you want to know what's going on, right?

RHYTHM BEYOND METER

AND NOW FOR the payoff. We've been talking about meter, but what really matters is rhythm, the beat we feel in poetry. Sometimes meter provides that, of course, but there are other ways to lay down a beat. One of our finest—and first—exponents of nonmetrical rhythm is Walt Whitman, as here, in section XI of *Song of Myself* (1855):

> *Twenty-eight young men bathe by the shore,*
> *Twenty-eight young men and all so friendly;*
> *Twenty-eight years of womanly life and all so lonesome.*

> *She owns the fine house by the rise of the bank,*
> *She hides handsome and richly drest aft the blinds of the*
> *window.*

> *Which of the young men does she like the best?*
> *Ah the homeliest of them is beautiful to her.*

Metrically, this passage is all over the map. The first line begins as trochees, "Twén-tĭ-éight yŏung," but then slides into an iamb, "mĕn báthe," but then concludes with an anapest, "bĭ thĕ shóre." We might even see that as twin anapests, "yŏung mĕn báthe bĭ thĕ shóre," which leaves the stressed "eight" standing on its own. The next line follows a similar pattern, but line three blows any expectations out of the water.

So what works for managing rhythm here? Several things take place. First, that favorite Whitman strategy, repetition. Beginning those first three lines with the same three syllables launches the poem forward. True, the third line upends what we thought we knew, that "twenty-eight" would be followed by an unstressed syllable followed by a stressed ("young MEN"). Instead, the number is followed by a stressed syllable, "YEARS," which brings us up short. Clearly, all the metrical knowledge in the world will not avail us.

Why, you ask? Because Whitman cares not about meter but about rhythm. Rather than sticking to an ordained metrical pattern, he is using other stylistic features to impart a sense of rhythm, of music if you will, to his poem. Repetition is one obvious example of such a feature. Those first two lines begin with "Twenty-eight young men," imparting a sort of rolling gait to the beginning. This sort of stacking of repeated phrases is more common in oratory, whether political or religious, than in poetry (although it is far from unknown). You can take speeches by nineteenth-century Daniel Webster or twenty-first-century Barack Obama or sermons by colonial preacher Jonathan Edwards or Martin Luther King, Jr. some two hundred years later and see how this phenomenon plays out rhetorically and sonically.

Another feature is *alliteration*, words repeating the same opening sound in succession, as in "bathe by" in line one or "hides handsome" in line five. As with any technique, alliteration can easily become heavy-handed, but a few short instances can work magic. A related feature is *consonance*, the repetition of consonant sounds in close proximity, although not necessarily occupying the same position within words. We see this in the woman's introduction in line three, "woman*l*y *l*ife and a*ll* so *l*onesome." Four different uses of *l* in three different positions: initial in "life" and "lonesome," terminal in "all," and penultimate in "womanly" (saved from the end by a vowel). At the same time, he reuses the related sounds *m* and *n*, which vary only by our lips being closed with one and open with the other, in "wo*m*a*n*ly" and "lo*n*eso*m*e." And he likes anapests here, especially to end his lines, as in "bĭ thĕ shóre," "thĕ fĭne hóuse bĭ thĕ ríse ŏf thĕ bánk," to achieve his desired effects.

Leaves of Grass offers hundreds, maybe thousands, of examples of these and other strategies to create rhythm, with scarcely a regular metrical line to be had. Whitman is making it up as he goes, this business of rhythm. With every new section of his great poem, he must ask himself three questions: What is the music of this part? How can I create it? And what effects will it accomplish? Far easier, of course, to fall back on the tried and true, the traditional metrical forms handed to him by Chaucer and Shakespeare and Wordsworth.

You know what this means, don't you? This is an earthquake, even if it's nearly impossible to sense seismic activity 150-plus years on. Since the time of Geoffrey Chaucer (who died in 1400),

English language poetry has built its castle on an iambic founda-
tion, and here comes this American upstart shaking it to smither-
eens. That sound you hear? That's the rumbling of the first truly
modern poet.

American poetry has been rumbling and shaking ever since.
Does that mean that the Yanks have a better sense of rhythm than the
Brits? Not really (you have only to read Ted Hughes to know that), but
it might be possible to argue that they have more experience and su-
perior early examples. I have long maintained that modern American
poetry grows directly (either by affinity or opposition) from Whit-
man. Modern British poetry, by contrast, grows from seeds planted
by two experts at traditional, closed-form poetics, Thomas Hardy and
William Butler Yeats. Whole schools of poetry, from the pre-WWI
Georgian poets to the fifties' Movement poets, have openly expressed
indebtedness to the terse, controlled verse of Hardy, while more or less
everyone else had to go through his or her Yeats period when starting
out. Even someone as unlike the master as Philip Larkin started out
writing bad imitations of Yeats before being part of the Hardy-esque
Movement. Americans, meanwhile, have not only Whitman to look
to but also a couple of other sprung-from-the-soil originals: Langston
Hughes and E. E. Cummings.

OTHER BASES FOR RHYTHM

LANGSTON HUGHES'S FIRST published poem, "The Negro Speaks of
Rivers," is quite Whitmanesque in the mix of long and short lines as
well as its repetition of key phrases, as in its first two lines:

> *I've known rivers:*
> *I've known rivers ancient as the world and older than*
> *the flow of human blood in human veins.*

The repeated initial three words in line two—along with the stacked prepositional phrases, "as the world," "than the flow," "of human blood," "in human veins"—creates an initial rhythm that organizes the sound of the rest of the poem:

> *My soul has grown deep like the rivers.*
>
> *I bathed in the Euphrates when dawns were young.*
> *I built my hut near the Congo and it lulled me to sleep.*
> *I looked upon the Nile and raised the pyramids above it.*
> *I heard the singing of the Mississippi when Abe Lincoln went down to New Orleans, and I've seen its muddy bosom turn all golden in the sunset.*
>
> *I've known rivers:*
> *Ancient, dusky rivers.*
>
> *My soul has grown deep like the rivers.*
> (1921)

The verbs change in those middle lines, but the pattern, "I [verb]" followed by some aspect of the river mentioned, remains the same. As with Whitman, those repetitions to start lines create a rhythm of their own. Again, the prepositional phrases run throughout the four lines from "in the Euphrates" to "in the sunset." Each one of those both deepens and rings changes on their use in line two. How? We know, even if we can't name them, the cadence of a prepositional phrase, the three- or four-word group following "in" or "on" or their numerous cousins: preposition-article-noun, as in "Under the Boardwalk," one of the great musical uses of the form. They are encoded into our understanding of how English sounds; merely to hear a preposition is to prepare ourselves for the rest of a very familiar pattern.

Even more to the point of our discussion, Hughes did three things that contributed to American poetry's sense of rhythm. First, he introduced African American dialect as something other than as a source of "local color" on the one hand or derisive humor on the other. When Hughes employs Black English, he does so to establish an authentic voice for some black experience and to find the musicality of that voice.

The mother in "Mother to Son," for instance, details her hardships metaphorically from her opening statement that "Life for me ain't been no crystal stair," following through with a catalog of challenges in the guise of issues with a more real-life stairway from tacks to splinters to broken treads, all the while asserting that she refuses to give up or stop climbing however difficult the endeavor. This use of a poetic *conceit*, a metaphor that extends throughout a poem and controls its imagery, is as sophisticated as anything by those seventeenth-century masters of the device, the so-called Metaphysical poets such as John Donne and Andrew Marvell, but it is accomplished with the very unpretentious language of a downtrodden African American woman. Hughes had his critics, including some in the black community who associated dialect with derogatory depictions of African Americans in minstrel shows and other forms of popular, usually white, entertainment. His vision, however, would ultimately win out among poets and writers of the second half of the twentieth century from Amiri Baraka to Ishmael Reed to Toni Morrison, who would further explore the musicality of the speech of their people. He was, after all, the inheritor of the traditions of both Walt Whitman and his great predecessor as poet of the African American experience, Paul Laurence Dunbar. That he would take Whitman's example of sympathy for and understanding of common people and marry that to his own racial community is almost inevitable.

Hughes's second source of rhythm in his poems is, unsurprisingly, the black church. He often punctuates his poems with and even organizes around such explosions of faith as "Glory! Hallelujah!" and "Sweet Jesus!" Such expressions are not unknown in white churches, of course, but among preachers and congregations of Hughes's experience, those exclamations would be a regular feature of the service. Again, he uses those outbursts in his own way, as likely to populate a poem about social injustice or a beautiful woman as one having to do with salvation. His poems may take the form of someone speaking in church, and those speakers' language will inform the rhythm of the poems.

His third great contribution lies in his exploration of the poetic possibilities of jazz and blues. Of course, many poets and lyricists have written *for* blues or jazz songs. He was not the only poet to attempt to capture the syncopation of jazz or the rhythmic structure of blues (numerous writers of the Harlem Renaissance were doing the same thing in the twenties), but he may have been the most widely read. And why not? He burst on the scene at virtually the same historical moment as Louis Armstrong, one of the first crossover stars of jazz, and his poetry is as infectious and lively as an Armstrong performance. He can write a straightforward twelve-bar blues as in "Po' Boy Blues" or something much more complex as in "The Weary Blues" (1926), in which the actual blues lines often appear in quotation marks, while the longer, more sinuous lines contain elements of the blues but refuse to hold still for any neat categorization, something more like jazz: improvisational, rhythmically syncopated, free-flowing:

> *Droning a drowsy syncopated tune,*
> *Rocking back and forth to a mellow croon,*
> *I heard a Negro play.*
> *Down on Lenox Avenue the other night*
> *By the pale dull pallor of an old gas light*
> *He did a lazy sway . . .*
> *He did a lazy sway . . .*
> *To the tune o' those Weary Blues.*

With his ebony hands on each ivory key
  He made that poor piano moan with melody.
   O Blues!
  Swaying to and fro on his rickety stool
  He played that sad raggy tune like a musical fool.
   Sweet Blues!
  Coming from a black man's soul.
   O Blues!

"We can find our own way," his poems assert, "showing our own people in our own language, celebrating our cultural heritage." This passage, lines nine through sixteen, captures that moment from the piano moaning to the "rickety stool" to the "raggy tune," two phrases I've yet to find in Shakespeare or Milton. His example would be followed by later "jazz poets" as otherwise different as Baraka and Beat poets Jack Kerouac and Lawrence Ferlinghetti. Once Hughes showed the world what could be done with actual music, especially popular music, in poetry, pretty much anything was possible.

The third shining example for American poets seeking their own rhythms comes from the utterly strange yet oddly familiar word-bender, E. E. Cummings:

Buffalo Bill 's
defunct
     who used to
     ride a watersmooth-silver

                         stallion
and break onetwothreefourfive pigeeonsjustlikethat

                                    Jesus

he was a handsome man
                    and what i want to know is
how do you like your blue-eyed boy
Mister Death

First published in 1922, this is a tiny poem, something we see more clearly if we print it in a more conventional arrangement:

> *Buffalo Bill's defunct*
> *who used to ride*
> *a water-smooth-silver*
> *stallion and break*
> *one-two-three-four-five pigeons*
> *just like that*
>
> *Jesus, he was a handsome man*
>
> *and what I want to know is*
> *how do you like your blue-eyed boy*
> *Mister Death*

In this case, page placement is as much a part of rhythm as the pattern of the words. Yes, the natural speaking style and the rat-a-tat delivery "onetwothreefourfive" and "justlikethat" have something to do with it. But it is hard to ignore the pauses enforced by the spatial leaps, either down the page, as in the break between "Buffalo Bill 's" and "defunct," which occupies a line all its own, or across the page, as when "stallion" seems marooned on an island or "Jesus" lurks out near the right margin. Cummings speeds us up and slows us down by using spatial placement as punctuation. A semicolon slows us down; so do three inches of blank line.

A LONG TIME AGO, BEFORE YOU WERE BORN AND EVEN BEFORE I WAS, English poetry used a different rhythm. Okay, not English poetry as we understand it but Old English (although they had no idea of being "Old"). We need to be clear here that Old English doesn't mean Shakespeare (Early Modern English) and it doesn't even mean Chaucer (Middle English). Nope, we're talking about Anglo-Saxon before the Norman conquest brought a lot of French elements and made the language sound less like gargling. So, anywhere between the time the Angles and Saxons overran the native Britons (fifth through seventh centuries CE) and the Battle of Hastings in 1066. What we know about it from the handful of surviving works (under two hundred considered major or significant) is that it liked strong stresses, alliteration, and short lines, while it cared not a whit for rhyme. You doubt? Try the first three lines of *Beowulf*:

> *Hwæt. Wē Gārdena   in gēardagum,*
> > [LO, praise of the prowess of people-kings]
> *þēodcyninga,   þrym gefrūnon,*
> > [of spear-armed Danes, in days long sped,]
> *hū ðā æþelingas   ellen fremedon.*
> > [we have heard, and what honor the athelings won!]

The italic lines are the Old English original, which you can't read. The lines in roman are the translation by Francis B. Gummere from the Harvard Classics, the five-foot shelf of books (1910), which is only slightly better. What's an "atheling," anyway? There are several major features here besides the strange letters. First, note that each line is split in two; that break is called a *caesura*, a term we still use to indicate some sort of break (in modern cases, usually via punctuation) in the middle of a line. Second, the lines are highly alliterative. In line one, not only the g from "Gardena" but also the *rd* carry over into the second *half-line* (that's the surprisingly straightforward term) in "geardagum." The third element at work involves counting. Very low counting. Each half-line (or *diptych*) typically has two strong stresses, indicated in our example by the flat line above the vowel. Unstressed syllables don't count at all, so none of that "metrical foot" noise that has been troubling your dreams. So, count to two, ignore the other syllables, and it's all good.

So why should you care? Well, every once in a great while, some poet takes it into his or her head to get back to basics. Not common, but the results can be spectacular. In the early nineteen seventies Seamus Heaney undertook to write poems dealing with both the Northern Irish contemporary conflict and the ancient past in something very like the half-line of Anglo-Saxon poetry. His success in conventional English versification had been somewhat vexed in his early volumes, yet he was unwilling to abandon formal verse altogether. Then, following the outbreak of sectarian violence in 1969, which became known as the Troubles, Heaney decided to marry the current climate of violence, earlier Viking raiders and settlers (who founded Dublin, among other acts), and some very old-fashioned poetics.

It worked stunningly. Here he is explaining that artistic choice in "Bone Dreams" (1975):

> *I push back*
> *through dictions,*
> *Elizabethan canopies,*
> *Norman devices,*
>
> *the erotic mayflowers*
> *of Provence*
> *the ivied latins*
> *of churchmen*
>
> *to the scop's*
> *twang, the iron*
> *flash of consonants*
> *cleaving the line.*

He depicts each of these past linguistic and poetic practices in the language and form of the last one; a scop is an Anglo-Saxon performer of poetry who is actually a creation of, um, Anglo-Saxon poetry. That is, he seems to have existed only as a depiction of the poet-performer *in* Anglo-Saxon poems. No contemporaneous documents exist confirming the existence in the real world, and we know that the poems were *written*, not recited, in the first instance.

Heaney is not scrupulous about having two stresses in every line, but the effect—heavy alliteration, short lines, hard consonants—absolutely captures the spirit of the original. So does his fondness for kennings, those compound nouns that describe a third thing, like "whale-road" for the sea. They seem exotic when we hear originals, but we use kennings all the time, as in our "fender-bender" for a minor accident. English, like other Germanic languages, is tailor-made for jamming nouns together as a way of enriching expression. Notable in this poem is his exploration of "ban-hus" ("bone-house"), a kenning that might seem to suggest an ossuary or charnel house but actually refers to the human body, which "houses bones," however briefly. Heaney decides to take the "hus" portion literally and thereby treat the body as a house of sorts, replete with walls, roof, and furnishings. In so doing, he acknowledges the tradition while pushing an ironic, postmodern understanding of it. This section (like the others a set of four spaced quatrains, something distinctly not Anglo-Saxon in origin) could double as an emblem of Heaney's approach to the distant past in *North*.

Here's the wild thing about the Heaney experiment: his adherence to what he elsewhere calls the "iambic drums" improves. A lot. When he emerges from what we might call his Viking period and returns to more conventional versification in *Field Work* (1979) and *Station Island* (1984), he displays a level of comfort with metered verse that sometimes eludes him in his earlier work. From this point forward, he marries the rhythms in his head to the metrical march of his lines as if he were born to do it. That's the main point about rhythm, isn't it—getting what one imagines onto the page or into the listener's ear seamlessly and naturally?

There are as many paths to that particular waterfall as there are poets. Some, like Frost, are such natural masters of meter that it disappears into the rhythms of speech almost entirely. Some, like Whitman, chart new courses to express their own rhythmic sense in original ways. And some, like Heaney, pursue their own innovations or borrow from other traditions in order to achieve comfort in their own. How poets reach their own rhythmic signatures is always a story unique to them, and we readers respond to both the journey and the arrival.

5

The Long (or Short) Gray Line

S O NOW WE KNOW THAT LINES OF POEMS ARE MADE UP OF METRI-cal feet (or not) and arranged in patterns (or not) to achieve spe-cific effects (I'm fairly sure this one applies universally). Admittedly, that's not much to go on. So here's the question: once words are ar-ranged into lines, what are they supposed to do? I spent a number of years in a writers' group with several friends. There were poets, fiction writers, memoirists—and me. What I added to the mix, aside from some dubious fiction, was one of the mysteries of the group, but it all seemed to work. And here is one thing I discovered fairly quickly. When discussing poems, we spent an inordinate amount of time on the question of line length: Why do you break the line here and not, say, over there? Are you looking for a specific rhythm in the line or the absence or even subversion of rhythm? And most of all, what do you want this line to do?

That's always the real question: *What do you want this line to do?*

This question sounds like something that would only apply to *free* or *open* or nonmetrical verse, and of course it does matter there. But it also applies to metrical verse. Sure, the line has to work out correctly; if you're writing iambic hexameter and your line suddenly works out to have seven rather than six beats, you've got yourself a problem.

But we allow a certain amount of liberty—as we discussed, *poetic license*—to arrange words in ways that are not common in prose, precisely so that desired poetic effects can be achieved. These decisions, logically enough, involve some very technical and sometimes dry matters. Does the poet want a natural word order, for instance, that will involve, say, a comma or semicolon at the end of the line, or a slightly convoluted order that will allow the line to end freely with no punctuation (what is called an enjambed line)?

In other words, the poet has to decide to do this rather than something else that might be almost equally plausible:

> *April is the cruelest month, breeding*
> *Lilacs out of the dead land, mixing*
> *Memory and desire, stirring*
> *Dull roots with spring rain.*
> *Winter kept us warm, covering*
> *Earth in forgetful snow, feeding*
> *A little life with dried tubers.*

Almost. It might be possible to end every line at the comma, so that we see:

> *April is the cruelest month,*
> *Breeding lilacs out of the dead land,*
> *Mixing memory and desire,*
> Etc.

Indeed, many lesser poets would likely do that. But this isn't a lesser poet; this is T. S. Eliot beginning *The Waste Land* (1922), and he knows he needs something to propel readers forward into this daunting poem full of unexplained allusions and untranslated quotes, to say nothing of its sudden leaps from place to place and time to time. He casts about and finds that the answer is . . . participles. Seriously? Participles? Yes, present participles, those magical little verb forms ("-ing" words, in this case) that end every line lacking a period: "breeding," "mixing," "stirring," "covering," "feeding." Residing at the beginnings of lines, they simply open participial phrases that are contained by those lines. At the *ends* of lines, they create suspense: What is April breeding, what was winter covering, and with what? My alternatives just lie there, inert; Eliot's lines drive across the line break, vaulting us over the gap as we seek answers to questions we didn't know we had.

Here's the point: grammatically and semantically, nothing changes from one version to the other. As sentences, the lines read and mean exactly the same thing. What changes is the reader's relation to the poem. Eliot causes us to become more active; each of those participles acts as a springboard from which we dive ahead toward the next surprise. That is what well-placed line breaks, at their best, can accomplish. Obviously, not every enjambed line will have the propulsive force of Eliot's. We should understand, rather, that there is (or should be) a reason for choosing to either end-stop or enjamb a line, and that there are always consequences connected with that choice, whatever it is.

That choice, in this instance, arises from an open-form or free verse poem, but it presents the same issues for traditional, closed-form poets. If we look at poems from the last chapter, we can see the logic of other choices. Here's Longfellow again:

> *By the shore of Gitche Gumee,*
> *By the shining Big-Sea-Water,*
> *At the doorway of his wigwam,*
> *In the pleasant Summer morning,*
> *Hiawatha stood and waited.*

What, every line end-stopped? As you can probably guess, this can't go on indefinitely. The result, after a few thousand lines, would be a little choppy, yes? But just for now, for getting this section started, it works. Each line here is a self-contained prepositional phrase, until the final line, which is an independent clause, a sentence that can stand on its own. The first four lines simply identify where Hiawatha did his standing and waiting: by the Big Lake, in his doorway, at a certain season and time of day. And it is customary when stacking prepositional phrases to separate them by commas.

Could Longfellow pull an Eliot here, maybe putting the prepositions on the previous lines? No. First of all, it simply isn't in his nature. A chickadee can't become a hawk. More to the point, however, the prepositions don't lend themselves to that sort of separation. I suppose you can have a "by" on the line before its noun, "by / The shining Big-Sea-Water," but it comes across as just dumb, and Longfellow is anything but that. More to the point, the single-syllable prepositions provide the downbeat for the first trochee, so their presence up front is essential.

Very different approaches, then, yet both instances possess that sense of inevitability that characterizes great poetry: "Of course it is like that; how else could it be?"

SOMEWHAT FREER VERSE

YOU KNOW WE'RE talking about literature, right, poetry being one of the founding members? And one of the rules of literature is that there are always exceptions. Even the exceptions have exceptions. So you shouldn't be too shocked to discover that the whole metered poetry business has some opt-outs. *Free verse* would be one of the obvious examples. "Free verse" is a not-terribly-accurate term for the sort of *open-form* poetry (many critics of it spoke of it as formless, but that's not necessarily true) that declined to be governed by rules of line and meter and stanza (the rule-governed type being called in this pairing *closed-form*). Taking nineteenth-century Walt Whitman as spiritual father, the free verse movement or impulse took off in a big way in the twentieth century, so much so that in the 1980s I was told by someone who should have known better that she couldn't really handle contemporary English poetry because whenever she saw poems with traditional versification (the closed-form type), she assumed they were parodies or jokes. I can promise you that even at his jokiest, sneaky-sly best, Philip

Larkin means business. So free verse or open-form poetry is one sort of reaction against the prevailing trend of seven or so centuries.

Free verse found its footing during the days of Imagism in the mid-1910s. That movement sought to cut the flab out of poetry by focusing strictly on the presentation of an image, as in one of its most famous poems (1923):

The Red Wheelbarrow

> *so much depends*
> *upon*
>
> *a red wheel*
> *barrow*
>
> *glazed with rain*
> *water*
>
> *beside the white*
> *chickens.*

There's really no inherent reason for those stanzas not to be single lines: "glazed with rain water" reads at least as well as "glazed with rain / water." And there is certainly no metrical imperative at work here. We might make the argument that each first line has two beats, each second only one. But is it true? Is that very first line, "So much depends" to be read as "Só mŭch dĕ-pénds" or "Só múch dĕ-pénds"? I incline toward the latter. And beyond that, those stressed syllables aren't offset by unstressed syllables in a regular metrical pattern. So let's think about what is gained by arranging it the way Williams does.

For one thing, this more vertical arrangement causes the poem to last just a little longer. Each one of those line endings forces our eye to travel down the page, and that takes time. Yes, it's fractional, but fractions count. Then, too, those line breaks introduce drama. Suspense, even. The drama might be less suspense than tension between an expectation he has set up and the thing he delivers. In the third "stanza," "rain" does not have to be followed by "water," although we might well expect that. Could be "droplets" or "sheen" or something of the sort, although, this being Williams, there is every likelihood that the plainspoken "water" is the answer. The real payoff is in the fourth stanza. Would you be expecting "chickens" when the card was pulled away in the big reveal? This could easily be a four-line poem, and even then, none of the lines would contain over six syllables. Yet by playing line breaks against readers' expectations, Williams creates something new and very surprising. And, as history will have it, very famous. Not exactly Sonnet 73, but it serves its creator's purpose as well as that sonnet serves Shakespeare's.

So that's one way to wave bye-bye to metrical feet.

But only one. Perhaps you're a poet who wants to get beyond all those iambs and trochees and such but who still wants the challenge of working within restrictions. What then? How about counting syllables? The haiku and related forms, thought exotic not that long ago, are instances of strict syllabic verse, and we have grown accustomed to them. Since the Middle Ages, French poets have practiced *syllabic verse*, which is to say, they have counted syllables exactly. Whereas Anglophone poets sometimes play fast and loose with added (or omitted) syllables, especially of the unstressed variety, the Francophone have been held to a more exacting standard. Happily, we're talking here about poems in English, where, especially in the twentieth century, poets can make their own rules. Now, French poems are overwhelmingly (from a historical perspective) written in either ten- or twelve-syllable lines, which is fine for them. But if you were a young American poet in the nineteen teens, and if you were something of a freethinker in matters of poetics, you might decide to reject three things: standard English metrical verse, free verse (where almost no rules apply), and French assumptions about how syllabic verse is supposed to behave. You might just do that, as Marianne Moore does:

The Fish

> wade
> through black jade.
> Of the crow-blue mussel-shells, one keeps
> adjusting the ash-heaps;
> opening and shutting itself like
>
> an
> injured fan.

That is the opening stanza of "The Fish" (1921) plus the first two lines of the second. I couldn't very well leave you with an unfinished sentence, could I? We'll talk about the stanza structure a bit later, when we move on to such matters. For now, however, I just want to focus on the line lengths. First, let's grant that each stanza has five lines, something you can't yet tell since you have only part of the poem. And all five lines are distinct. The first line has one syllable; the second one, three; the third, nine; the fourth, six; and the fifth, eight. So that's the first stanza. And the second one? 1–3–9–6–8. Same with the third, fourth, and so on. When you see the whole poem on the page, after a moment or so your eye adjusts and tells you, "Hey, these all look alike." That's because, I think, of the staggered starts: the first two are flush left, the second two indented three spaces, the fifth indented another three. Some people claim that the ragged beginnings of lines emulate the rough face of a coral reef, which is the subject that the poem really describes.

Admittedly, syllabic verse is a fairly small subset of all poetry in English, but that doesn't mean it hasn't been done or won't be done again in the future. As with most things artistic, we are limited only by the range of our own imaginations.

RADICAL SHIFTS

IN HIS FIRST four books, W. S. Merwin followed conventional, even classical models for poems, and he was very good at them. His first volume, *A Mask for Janus* (1952), won the Yale Younger Poets Award, and he received numerous fellowships and grants. *The Drunk in the Furnace* (1960) seemed like the arrival of a major voice in American poetry; it was, but not in the way it promised. With his fifth volume, *The Moving Target* (1963), he abandoned punctuation. And with it, capitalization, aside from the first words of poems and the occasional proper noun. Then, having turned his back on punctuation, he never turned back. Remember our earlier discussion of how to read poems, where I told you to read sentences; that sentences, not lines, were the basic unit of meaning in poetry? That injunction relied on one certainty: we can recognize the contours of a sentence and can therefore know where a sentence begins and ends, and the basis for that knowledge is a single punctuation mark, the period. Oh, sure, you can end sentences with a couple of others, but that's the one that sets the standard. So here's the question: If you remove the period from your writing, and with it the various siblings and cousins that cause us to pause, proceed, and stop in our reading, how do we know when a statement has ended? In other words, if you don't have sentences in the normal sense, what do you have? The line:

Early One Morning

> *Here is Memory walking in the dark*
> *there are no pictures of her as she is*
> *the coming day was never seen before*
> *the stars have gone into another life*
> *the dreams have left with no sound of farewell*
> *insects awake flying up with their feet wet*
> *trying to take the night along with them*
> *Memory alone is awake with me*
> *knowing that this may be the only time*

This poem is from his 2016 volume, *Garden Time*. That's sixty-four years of poetry books, which in itself boggles the mind. Most of the volume was composed at a time of failing eyesight when Merwin had to dictate poems to his wife, making the achievement all the more remarkable. "Early One Morning" represents his late mode quite well: clear, direct, simple, unadorned even, yet touched with magic. "Memory" behaves like a Greek goddess. Like her ancient predecessor, Mnemosyne, she is female, and attendant on one party only (at least from his perspective); there are no pictures of her "as she is," so she can only be seen as perceived by the speaker.

Excepting of the lack of punctuation, the poem is quite conventional. Each of the nine lines has ten syllables, giving it a familiar look. Those syllables sometimes group around four beats, sometimes around five. Merwin is not always quite this regular in line structure, but a great many poems do adhere to a consistent length. Most lines are more or less self-contained statements, with two (lines six and eight) spilling over onto the next. This format permits him to show what he can accomplish with short, simple statements. For instance, "the coming day was never seen before" exudes a sneaky profundity; our first impulse may be to slough it off as obvious, but if we recall that this is a poem in which Memory stalks the house, we realize that she has no access to that day—yet. And those last two lines contain a minor mystery: Is it Memory or the speaker who knows that "this may be the only time"? Syntax suggests the former, but there is just enough ambiguity in the lines to leave the matter open.

Critics could have been forgiven for dismissing Merwin's eschewing of punctuation as just another literary stunt, akin to novelist Henry Green dropping nearly all use of definite and indefinite articles ("the," "a," "an") from his second novel, *Living*. Unlike Green, however, Merwin never went back nor looked back, so that it went from an experiment to a mode of poetic being for him. Indeed, the practice became so identified with him that it would be hard for anyone else to take it up without seeming derivative.

BEFORE WE FINISH, WE MUST ACKNOWLEDGE THAT THERE IS A TINY but determined body of poetry for which this discussion holds no meaning because they have no lines. Our customary term for such works is *prose poems*, although the writers who commit them are as likely as not to disavow the name. Perhaps the earliest instances come from the *haibun*, a form that blended prose elements with traditional haiku (you know, 5–7–5), which was developed by the seventeenth-century Japanese poet Basho. In the West, the form originated in nineteenth-century Europe, where poets such as French Symbolists Charles Baudelaire and Arthur Rimbaud experimented with its possibilities. It makes appearances at intervals throughout the twentieth century, often among writers who reject conventional literary assumptions, as with Beat Generation writers Jack Kerouac, Allen Ginsberg, and William S. Burroughs. Three notable volumes from the nineteen seventies and eighties are Robert Bly's *The Morning Glory*, Geoffrey Hill's *Mercian Hymns*, and Charles Simic's Pulitzer Prize-winning *The World Doesn't End*. Bly's book began as an overt homage to Basho, so he was obviously accepting of the term, and Charles Simic never disavowed it, but Hill, ever the contrarian, strenuously rejected it, claiming the thirty numbered sections were "versets of rhythmical prose." *Versets* are small verses, particularly those drawn from Scripture. Hill's poems are about the mythical King Offa of the English Midlands—sometimes mixing in more modern stories—and are usually brief, wry, even sardonic, but for all that still frequently moving. None of those poems care a farthing for line length or structure.

All of this is a rather roundabout way of saying that lines are what you make of them. They can be long or short, metered or not, rhymed or not. However they appear, they are the critical feature separating poetry from prose (prose poems notwithstanding), the essential building blocks of verse. If we wish to honor the effort a poet makes, we need to look carefully at the way she marshals her lines.

6

Our Word Is Our Bond

———————

IT WILL NOT HAVE ESCAPED YOUR ATTENTION THAT LITERATURE IS made of words. Words matter in novels, but not in quite the same way that they do in lyric poetry. A poem of the sort we're talking about might run from a couple to a couple hundred lines and contain somewhere between a dozen and a very few thousand words, fewer than the difference between Dickens's *David Copperfield* and *Bleak House*. It doesn't take a genius to figure out that those words are likely to count for more than those in a Victorian triple-decker, if only because their count is so small.

I stress here that this level of attention to words is a feature of *lyric* poetry. Dramatic or epic verse forms often have a somewhat looser relation to word choice—if not quite like novels, then leaning in that direction. Even then, assuming written and not oral epics, words matter. Greatly. And you know what the problem is with words? Poetry doesn't own them. There is no privileged language of poetry—or any literature, for that matter—so poets have to make do with language that has been debased and devalued by many kinds of use and abuse.

Any word you seek for your poem will have already been used in ways that cloud its meaning or steal its precision or sometimes render it unusable. A writer before, say, 1970 or thereabouts could use a phrase like "hearts are gay" without a second thought as to clarity or intent. After the word's appropriation by the gay pride movement, however, the word carries a different charge from anything it ever had before. The transformation came about faster and more comprehensively than any linguistic change most of us who lived through it can remember. That's okay; "gay" in the new sense gets a lot more use than it did formerly, and language inevitably shifts to adapt to altered social conditions. A writer today, I suppose, can still use "gay" in the manner of Cole Porter or P. G. Wodehouse, but there will be consequences; the audience has changed its perceptions. Most alterations are more incremental and stem from less noble endeavors. Think about how official documents deaden language. The point of a regulation or a letter from your insurance company is not to enliven anything but to state as impersonally as possible something the reader may take very personally. Propaganda routinely uses language to obscure rather than clarify motives while misrepresenting events or actions.

This quandary—how do we use something so devalued as language as the medium for art—is nothing new. The French Symbolist poets—Paul Verlaine, Stéphane Mallarmé, Arthur Rimbaud, and Co.—decried this dilemma in the late nineteenth century. Geoffrey Hill (1932–2016), in an essay whose title I have stolen for a chapter in this book, "Redeeming the Time," says that poetry inevitably struggles against "the inertial drag of speech. Language gravitates and exerts a gravitational pull." This particular statement is made in the context of rhythm, but he amends it to include words themselves, in another essay whose title is also the title of this chapter, ominously including the word "bond," suggesting both allegiance or trust (to swear a bond, to be bonded) and captivity (to be held in bondage). In each case, he argues that language provides resistance against the work of the poet and that in struggling to overcome that resistance poets achieve their art. This linguistic resistance is likely the source of the impulse in poetry for at least the last century to "make it new," in Pound's phrase, to make it fresh, different, or sometimes merely strange. From Williams's "The Red Wheelbarrow" and T. S. Eliot's *The Waste Land* to

Sylvia Plath's "Daddy" and Craig Raine's "A Martian Sends a Postcard Home," modernist and postmodernist poetry have tried to make us see with new eyes and, more importantly, hear with new ears.

One element of the poetic obsession with words is what we term *diction*, by which we mean the words alone and in combination, the modes of phrasing, and the uses of metaphor and simile that a poet settles upon. For example, at the end of the previous sentence, I used "settles upon" rather than some other words meaning the same thing. It has the advantage of being grammatically preferred, historically speaking, to "settles on," which may sound more modern to some ears. My version may sound perfect to you, or it may seem just a little stiff; your response will reveal something about your own reading and linguistic experience as well as my choices.

Words have numerous components that attract our attention. We tend to think in terms of meaning, or what we speak of as their *semantic* level. There is also the *syntactic* level, which is to say, how the words nestle in among their neighbors. A third level is the aesthetic, which can take a couple of forms. Written language can involve us in visual aesthetics. How does a word look on the page? Is it tall on the ends and short in the middle, or the reverse, or more random in appearance? Is there a clot of consonants in it somewhere, and where?

What concerns us more frequently is language in the oral realm: How do the words sound? Light and airy? Sturdy and heavy? This aspect of diction, namely how they look and sound, is important. Writers in every language have a number of choices for words in any particular place in a statement, but English, a Germanic language, imports words from French, Latin, Greek, Hindi, Arabic, Spanish, Chinese, Japanese, Dano-Norwegian, Inuit, Algonquian, and just about any other language with which it comes in contact. It also has an annoying (or delightful, depending on your viewpoint) habit of simply making words up when the occasion arises, using those other languages, slang, techno-speak, and even acronyms as the basis for new words. As a result, the writer in English has a dizzying array of choices for most content words (those not "the," "an," "a," or various conjunctions and prepositions like "and" and "or" and "under" and "on"), and those choices will always convey a story. Is the word long or short? A traditional word dating back to Old English or a newer import? How new? Which language? Greek and Geek aren't the same, you know.

You don't have to be interested in poetry to see history at work in language. If you ever deal with a will—and it is a rare person who doesn't, at some point—you will see the phrase "give bequeath and devise." Why? Blame William the Conqueror. In 1066, William, Duke of Normandy, came across the English Channel and defeated English King Harold at the Battle of Hastings, thereby changing the world. If you never learn anything else about the history of the English language, know that date. It marks the beginning of the process of changing our language from something you can neither read nor understand, the purely Germanic language of Old English, to a Germanic language with a heavy overlay of French vocabulary. In practice, Germanic words are generally shorter, harsher, and regarded as cruder; French-origin words tend to be longer, softer, and more socially acceptable. Words from Latin are the long, legalistic sounding ones, but that's another story. After the Norman conquest, legal documents needed to be clear for both the native (okay, earlier conquerors) Anglo-Saxons and the newly installed Norman French speakers. "Give" and "bequeath," from Old English, worked for the first group, "devise," from Old French, for the second. These pairings remained long after the linguistic divide had vanished.

How does that work? Okay, in the realm of bodily functions, the euphemisms or formal terms are virtually always from Latin (think "fornication," "defecation," "urination"), while the rude terms are from either Old English (the first two) or Old French by way of Middle English (the third one). Don't pretend you don't know them. Oh, and four letters long. And you thought this stuff would be dull!

Want a reason to pay attention to word choice? In the midst of a typically plainspoken poem, Philip Larkin's "Church Going" (1955), the speaker refers to the church in question as an "accoutred frowsty barn." For someone whose native style is as unflashy as his, this is a spectacular mashup. "Accoutred" is from French, meaning something like "all decked out." "Frowsty," a word I have never seen from an American writer, is a nineteenth-century corruption of "frowsy," which in turn is a seventeenth-century British slang word of unknown origin, meaning musty or stale-smelling. And "barn" is good, plain English going back to good, plain Old English, when it meant the house that stored the barley. It is not, inevitably, a word we associate with churches. Nor are the others, come to think of it.

Poetic diction is a really big deal. In fact, the great critic Owen Barfield published an entire book on the subject called, shockingly, *Poetic Diction* (1928). His subtitle is *A Study in Meaning*, and his immediate goal is to examine how the poetic imagination deploys words and metaphor to create meaning. Barfield was part of the Inklings group that included C. S. Lewis and J. R. R. Tolkien, so of course there is more going on than mere literary criticism. In this case, he studies the history of diction in poetry for evidence of a sort of evolution of consciousness. We will limit ourselves here to the more obvious questions of how word choice and placement affects poems.

Wait a minute. You mean we're going to go crazy over a bunch of frills and ribbons?

Not at all. Diction ain't frilly, Buster. See what I did there? Nonstandard "ain't," colloquial mode of address with "Buster"; that's diction. And not the version I've mostly been using here.

So what is it, exactly?

Think of diction as four of the five *W*s of journalism: Who, What, When, Where, and How. All of which leads to Why, naturally enough. What words does the writer use; when and where does he drop them into sentences (or fragments); and how do those choices affect what we hear going on as we read? Ultimately, we want to figure out, as best we can, why the writer has made those choices, but that can only be achieved by a sort of literary reverse engineering. Wordsworth said that "we murder to dissect," but the reality is we dissect to understand. By the way, the patient usually survives.

We can read poetry and other documents—or think we can—

because words have more or less stable roles. Adjective may come before or after, but it is always going to be near neighbors with a *thing*, a noun or pronoun, and its function will be descriptive. We have no trouble understanding a movie title like *Ordinary People* or *Despicable Me* because we have seen and heard adjectives used this way all our lives. No need to know the word "adjective"; the function is clear long before any understanding of the parts of speech. Same thing with nouns and verbs, adverbs and conjunctions: they are mostly stable forms. Occasionally the culture picks up a noun and turns it into a verb, often to great consternation, as with "impact" in our own era or "share" in the sixteenth century, so long ago that we believe it has always been a verb as well as a noun. This sort of seismic activity in language goes on in all ages but rarely results in damage to buildings or livestock. Mostly, we live in the assurance that our language is built upon the rock.

WHAT PARTS OF SPEECH?

BUT WHAT HAPPENS when someone blows those certainties apart?

> *anyone lived in a pretty how town*
> *(with up so floating many bells down)*
> *spring summer autumn winter*
> *he sang his didn't he danced his did.*

Even if you had never seen the poem, if you know anything about E. E. Cummings, you're pretty sure as to the culprit. He has a well-earned reputation for verbing nouns and nouning verbs, but in this poem those are the least of his crimes. We'll talk about the whole poem in detail later, but for now, let's examine these first four lines, wherein he gives us most of the devices he will use in the poem to shake the foundations. The first line is comprehensible in word order, if not meaning. If we substitute more or less any personal pronoun or proper noun—

"he," "they," "Sam," "she"—the subject and verb work together just fine. So, too, with the problematic "how"; that position before "town" needs an adjective rather than an adverb: a pretty *farm* town, a pretty *suburban* town. You get the idea. "How"? Not so much. Like "anyone" at the beginning, it more or less invites us to substitute other possibilities precisely because it is so generic. "Anyone" usually calls for a "could" or a "might": *anyone could be forgiven, anyone might think,* anyone might concur that "anyone" does not play well with verbs in the simple past like "lived."

The second line throws word order out the window: "with up so floating many bells down." It may, or may not, mean something like "with so many bells floating up and then down," but as Cleanth Brooks pointed out decades ago, there is heresy in paraphrasing poetry. In any case, what matters is what the line itself says—and of course how it says it. Because it really matters that "so" comes, however improbably, between "up" and "floating." If it fell later, say, "floating many so bells down," it would not be the same at all. Can I say what that difference would be? Don't be silly. No one could. Because as written it says what it says. And is what we have.

The third line seems straightforward enough, "spring summer autumn winter," just like that. A little surprising, maybe, to have anything appear in correct, natural order in this poem, but it does. It recurs throughout the poem with different seasons in the initial spot, from spring to autumn and finally summer batting leadoff, but it maintains the order, suggesting the passage of time. But then order vanishes in a masterful instance of nouning verbs: "he sang his didn't he danced his did." Semantically, the line appears meaningless. Our ears tell us we need nouns for "didn't"/"did"; "sorrow"/"joy" would work, or even "ego"/"id." This reminds us, of course, that the clause is structurally perfect, only apparently nonsensical. If we take a little time to reflect, though, we may find some meaning after all. "Didn't" and "did" can suggest negation and affirmation or inaction and action or even nonbeing and being. If we listen for the sense imparted by the words rather than insisting on a traditional model, we see a host of possibilities for the line's meaning. In rejecting the words' function in favor of their potential implications, Cummings shifts the linguistic paradigms. That's good, because he will pursue that shift through the remainder of the poem, as we shall see later.

Before we leave this passage, it would be unfair not to admit that it is a whole lot of fun to say, even if you stumble. Maybe because you stumble. Stumbling is half the fun. Therein lies the secret to Cummings's charm: he leaves you baffled but smiling.

SPEAKING LIKE YOUR PEEPS

THE SOCIAL COMPACT can also be battered by the use of dialect. We know the expected words, the usual suspects; what we may not know are the words from another linguistic tradition, be it ethnic, regional, or national, even though it's all, ostensibly, English. Such usage might seem designed to limit a poem's availability to most readers, and it can have that effect. We have to explain, then, how Robert Burns remains one of the most popular poets in the English language. Do you know of any other poet whose birthday is an occasion for international celebration, other than possibly Shakespeare—or even whose birth date is known by the general public (January 25, in case you're not Scottish or Canadian)? Whose best-known poem is mangled by drunks each New Year's Eve? Try that with "Prufrock." A Burns poem in dialect will often feature many sections where we can almost find our way interspersed with moments of incomprehension, as in these two critical stanzas of "To a Mouse":

> *Thy wee-bit heap o' leaves an' stibble*
> *Has cost thee monie a weary nibble!*
> *Now thou's turn'd out, for a' thy trouble,*
>   *But house or hald,*
> *To thole the Winter's sleety dribble,*
>   *An' cranreuch cauld!*

> *But Mousie, thou art no thy-lane,*
> *In proving foresight may be vain;*
> *The best laid schemes o' Mice an' Men*
>   *Gang aft agley,*
> *An' lea'e us nought but grief an' pain,*
>   *For promis'd joy!*

The speaker has turned up a mouse's nest with his plow, resulting in an all-around calamity. The mouse needs the nest to survive the winter, while the human gains nothing by the destruction except a sense of guilt. The two stanzas focus on the salient point of desolation despite careful planning and economy. "The little heap of materials and supplies," the speaker says, "cost you plenty. But now you're turned out of your house even with all your effort, and winter's sleet and crushing cold will beset you." Most of that first stanza is manageable. We can more or less figure out "stibble" and "house or hald," and if we can't manage "to thole" on its own, we can figure out from "Winter's sleety dribble" that it's going to mean something like "endure." Which it does. But then what in the world are we to make of "cranreuch cauld"? If we've read a bit of Burns before, we may get that "cauld" is a phonetic rendering of our very own "cold." "Cranreuch," on the other hand, is beyond our ken. In fact, it is a Scots word for hoarfrost, the frozen form of dew. You can never get there on your own, but coupled with the context, you know it is something soul-crushing (and possibly bone-crunching) for the mouse.

The second stanza is fairly straightforward, excepting "lane" for "alone" or "on your own" and "Gang aft agley," for conventional English's "oftimes go awry," which is how it came down to me. Indeed, that may be the most comprehensible alien line in literature, because the culture has taught us what follows "The best laid schemes o' Mice an' Men." If there were any doubt, the last two lines complete the thought, "And lea'e us nought but grief an' pain / For promis'd joy!" We may not glean every morsel from the lines, but we can certainly follow the gist. We find ourselves rewarded with the many wry comments, not least of them his addressing of his victim as "Mousie," which invokes a curious sort of kinship between these two unequal strivers. Part of the joy of a Burns poem, for some readers, is precisely that alien element that dialect brings to the commonplace. Anyone who has turned over soil will have had the experience of uprooting some other creatures who have done us no harm, but we won't have produced our thoughts in such unearthly language.

Dialect poetry is always a vexed subject. How much is too much? Is it accurate depiction or caricature? Does it exclude outsiders unfamiliar with the dialect? What does it mean to move back and forth between dialect and Standard English? Paul Laurence Dunbar, who often used African American dialect in his poems, here chooses to write in mainstream English:

Compensation

> *Because I had loved so deeply,*
> *Because I had loved so long,*
> *God in His great compassion*
> *Gave me the gift of song.*
>
> *Because I have loved so vainly,*
> *And sung with such faltering breath,*
> *The Master in infinite mercy*
> *Offers the boon of Death.*

His dialect poems raised objections for possibly bringing the race into disrepute or reducing them to caricatures. But he wanted to reach multiple audiences, and when he wished to reach white readers, he knew how to produce Standard English. The first stanza of the poem sits as a sort of architectural epigraph on the facade of the Dayton (Ohio) Metro Library's main branch in Dunbar's hometown. I read it many times in my youth, inspired to know that a famous poet had come from my blue-collar community. The library wisely omits the second, rather less inspiring stanza. I include it here not as a source of study but as evidence, if such were needed, that Dunbar was fully capable of writing in Standard English. He may be better known for his dialect poems, which he called "Minors" in contrast to the Standard English "Majors," but those poems were controversial when he first published them and have never stopped being so.

So, then, words. Can't live with 'em, can't live without 'em. Wallace Stevens has a poem called "Men Made Out of Words," which could be the anthem, adjusted for gender, for poets everywhere. Stuck with the same lousy, degraded building blocks as lawyers and propagandists and writers of college regs and hashtaggers, they strive to make something new.

7

Rhyme Thyme

A NOTHER MAJOR CONSIDERATION IN THE POETIC USE OF WORDS IS, of course, rhyme. The decision to rhyme—and how and when to rhyme—will dictate much not only about the rhyming words but also about the arrangement of all the other words. We'll talk about rhyme schemes when we get around to discussing stanzas, but for now what we want to focus on is how words that end with the same or similar sounds (or sometimes look as if they should) create a kind of music. When someone talks about a rhyme, they usually mean an *end rhyme*. That makes sense; they are the most common and recognizable:

> *Tyger, tyger, burning* bright,
> *In the forests of the* night.

The first two lines of William Blake's "The Tyger" have the advantage of not only rhyming but also being a couplet, a rhyming pair right next to each other. Rhyming lines need not be that close to one another, and the patterns in which they rhyme can be quite complex, but for the moment, let's limit ourselves to the basic concept. Rhymes don't have to sit at the ends of lines; they can also happen within the line, where a word on the interior rhymes with the one at the end (or sometimes one in the next line), in which case we call them *internal rhymes*, exhibiting just how imaginative literary scholars can be. One frequently invoked instance of internal rhyme is Edgar Allan Poe's "The Raven," whose first line reads, "Once upon a midnight *dreary*, while I pondered, weak and *weary*." It's true: those are full chimes for each other. On the other hand, it feels a little like cheating. What Poe has done here is take rhyming short lines and lay them end to end so that his rhymes fall at the midpoint and the end rather than in couplets:

> *Once upon a midnight* dreary,
> *While I pondered, weak and* weary . . .

There's nothing wrong with laying the thing out as he does, and it has the advantage of killing fewer trees. Usually, however, internal rhymes are occasional things, as in the example below. Still, Poe's use does strike a sort of incantatory chord in his fevered verse.

End and internal rhymes are not mutually exclusive, as the witches of *Macbeth* remind us:

> *Double, double, toil and trouble,*
> *Fire burn and cauldron bubble.*

They sound nice. All sorts of fun is happening here. First, we have the internal rhyme (triplets!) in line one with "double, double" and "trouble," and then line two completes the end rhyme with "bubble." Moreover, in doubling "double," Shakespeare gives us an *identical rhyme*. That sort of repetition is usually frowned upon at the end of lines in English but much more acceptable internally, as here. Beyond that, these are *feminine rhymes*, meaning that two or more syllables rhyme. If we had lines ending instead with "trouble," and "rumble," that would still be a rhyme, if your standards aren't very high, because the last syllables rhyme even though the first ones do not. To be fair, we call that a *slant rhyme*, which means it only sort of rhymes but fulfills a purpose none the less.

Rhyme schemes come in all sorts of patterns, which can be put to all manner of uses. Let's say, for instance, that you want to write a long poem and get it to hang together as it meanders southward down page after page. You might want some sort of interlocking yet simple rhyme scheme. And you might decide that some white space would be a nice touch. In that case, you might try three-line stanzas, with the first and third lines rhyming. So where's the interlocking part come in? Carryover. If you take that second, as yet unrhymed line ending and use that rhyme as line four, it becomes the first line of the second stanza, which means that it also shows up in line three of that stanza, with an orphaned line ending in between. The resulting rhyme scheme will look like this: ABA-BCB-CDC-DED-EFE-FGF-GHG, and so on. Now here is where poets have it better than students of poetry: they never have to remember the lettering for the rhymes. Just establish the pattern and follow it down the page. It will work; you can tie a really long poem together with this pattern. How do we know? Because it's been around for a while. Dante Alighieri used it for his *Divine Comedy* in 1320. It found its way into English verse with lightning speed for the Middle Ages when Geoffrey Chaucer used it, still in the fourteenth century. The form, which is called *terza rima* (third rhyme, which just sounds dumb, hence the adherence to the Italian term), has been used by just about everybody down the centuries from John Milton to Percy Bysshe Shelley to T. S. Eliot to Thomas Hardy to W. H. Auden and on and on.

The *original* terza rima example is Dante's *The Divine Comedy*, which, if you're like me, you can't read. So how about something we *can* read? How about "Acquainted with the Night" by Robert Frost? Dante's work is an epic, a length the rhyme scheme is very well suited to to carry the reader along. This one, happily, is not an epic:

> *I have been one acquainted with the night.*
> *I have walked out in rain—and back in rain.*
> *I have outwalked the furthest city light.*

I have looked down the saddest city lane.
I have passed by the watchman on his beat
And dropped my eyes, unwilling to explain.

I have stood still and stopped the sound of feet
When far away an interrupted cry
Came over houses from another street,

But not to call me back or say good-bye;
And further still at an unearthly height,
One luminary clock against the sky

Proclaimed the time was neither wrong nor right.
I have been one acquainted with the night.

This is a fine poem, well worth a discussion about its construction and meaning, but for now, let's just concentrate on the rhyme scheme. And to do that, it's easiest if we abstract out the rhyming words:

Night	(A)
Rain	(B)
Light	(A)
Lane	(B)
Beat	(C)
Explain	(B)
Feet	(C)
Cry	(D)
Street	(C)
Good-bye	(D)
Height	(A)
Sky	(D)
Right	(A)
Night	(A)

At first glance, it might look like a regular ABAB rhyme scheme, but then we notice three things. First, that the rhyming words occur three times. Except, second, the A rhymes in lines one, three, eleven, thirteen, and fourteen. And, third, the reuse of the A rhyme at the end, and especially the A couplet at the end, which means this poem is not continuing.

What's that you say? A sonnet? How good of you to notice. Yes, there are fourteen lines here, iambic pentameter and everything. It is one of two very famous poems to eschew the Petrarchan and Shakespearean models for the sonnet and to make use of terza rima as the organizing principle. The other is Percy Bysshe Shelley's "Ode to the West Wind." For now, though, just the rhymes, ma'am. Or rimes. If it felt to you like alternating rhymes, that's good: you got the general feel. Where it differs from standard ABAB, however, is in the forward push provided by the interlocking quality that begins with lines two, four, and six ("rain"/"lane"/"explain") and continues throughout. Because there's always a *third* rhyme coming, our awareness of any particular rhyme is extended beyond our expectations. Having heard "rain," we're more or less satisfied when "lane" pops up, but then we get "explain" and it catches us off guard, elongating the experience ever so slightly. Think of this as primarily an auditory issue. The eye can perceive three similar words without issue, but we are acclimated to *hearing* rhymes in twos. If we get three, it changes our relationship to the poem. And the nature of the rhyme scheme, as we shall see a bit later, matters enormously to the organization of information in the poem.

NOW THEN, IF WE'RE GOING TO TALK ABOUT RHYMED VERSE, WE need something to compare it to, just so we know that it's special. That something is called *blank verse*. So what's that? "Blank," in this instance, is simply the going term for "unrhymed."

So in a chapter on rhyme you're talking about stuff that doesn't rhyme?

Yeah, pretty much the size of it. Rhymed and blank verse are actually more closely related than you might think. Let's begin by stipulating that we're not talking about *free verse*, which is also usually unrhymed, here. "Free" in this case would indicate an absence of normal rules of the road involving meter, line length, stanza arrangement, and overall regularity of composition. Blank verse, by contrast, follows the conventions with a single major exception: it doesn't rhyme.

The first use in English of blank verse seems to have been a translation of Virgil's *Aeneid* by Henry Howard, Earl of Surrey, published between 1554–7. And he may have done so for the best of reasons: the original didn't rhyme. Classical verse, whether Homer's Greek or Virgil's Latin, had no use for rhyme. Why that was, someone who actually knows the languages would have to say. Once the earl had shown us the way, poetry in English really embraced blankness. Most of Shakespeare's plays, like those of his immediate predecessor Christopher Marlowe (d. 1593), are in blank verse. John Milton's greatest work, *Paradise Lost* (1667), is written in unrhymed iambic pentameter, as are such Romantic-era poems as William Wordsworth's "Tintern Abbey," Samuel Taylor Coleridge's "This Lime-Tree Bower My Prison," John Keats's "Hyperion," and Shelley's "Prometheus Unbound." Modern poets as various as Wallace Stevens, W. B. Yeats, Robert Frost, and W. H. Auden have all used blank verse. There's a lot of it out there. How much? In *Poetic Meter and Poetic Form*, Paul Fussell estimated that "about three-quarters of all English poetry is in blank verse." So yes, a lot.

Not free. Blank. And here's the funny part: virtually all of that blank verse is in the metrical form Milton used, iambic pentameter. There's no Divine Ordinance decreeing this choice—which actually seems like no choice at all. Still, there it is. As common as iambic pentameter may be generally in English verse, it is as nothing compared to its ubiquity when said verse is unrhymed.

So does that mean that it all sounds alike? Not at all. The results are as varied as the practitioners of the form, from Shakespeare and Marlowe to Adrienne Rich and Robert Pinsky.

There is one fact, however, common to all writers of blank verse in all eras: they have to avoid rhymes. To clarify just a bit, they have to avoid end rhymes. Interior rhymes, as well as assonance and consonance and alliteration, are just fine. But once your plan for a blank sonnet becomes clear, the echo of a line with one of its near neighbors isn't a chime but the clang of a cracked bell. That's easy, you say? Try it sometime. There's an imp of the perverse (to use Poe's term) who will maliciously introduce rhyming words exactly where you don't want them. Writing rhyming poetry may be one of the hardest tasks in all of literature, but writing poetry that consciously—and conscientiously—avoids rhymes is a close second.

Which brings up a final point on blank verse. We tend to think of it as primarily a tool of the narrative poem or the stage drama, but it can take many forms. Yes, indeed, there are blank sonnets. Fourteen lines, possibly a separation between the initial octave and the closing sestet. The poet will have to work to signal that separation, however, because the traditional means, the ending of one rhyme scheme and the beginning of another, is not possible in a poem with no rhymes. So, too, with other forms: as long as rhyme isn't the main constituent element of the form, adapting it to unrhymed lines is possible. Sometimes it is possible anyway. Heaney has at least one instance of nonrhyming terza rima, which is a little odd when "rima" is its last name.

What does blank verse sound like? Almost anything you want it to. Here is the beginning of one of the great poems about thoughts and memories, William Wordsworth's "Tintern Abbey":

> *Five years have past; five summers, with the length*
> *Of five long winters! and again I hear*
> *These waters, rolling from their mountain-springs*
> *With a soft inland murmur.—Once again*

Do I behold these steep and lofty cliffs,
That on a wild secluded scene impress
Thoughts of more deep seclusion; and connect
The landscape with the quiet of the sky.

In truth, the full title is "Lines Composed a Few Miles above Tintern Abbey, On Revisiting the Banks of the Wye during a Tour. July 13, 1798." Whew! You see why we shorten it. If Hamlet is conducting an argument—fraught, sometimes violent—with himself in his soliloquys (also blank verse), Wordsworth is taking a stroll down memory lane. Which overlooks a river. Like the soliloquy, the poem, part ode, part interior monologue, is written in scrupulous decasyllabics, although it has a more relaxed approach to its still-dominant iambic pentameter—ten syllables, but not always five metrical feet. The soundscape is softer, more rounded. The first three lines, for instance, have almost no hard consonants, and those are in the middle or at the end of words. Consider, for instance, "Five years have past, five summers, with the length / Of five long winters!" The repeated "five" provides a sort of vibration of all those *f* and *v* sounds, which are further softened by the *m/n* sounds and sibilants, and the liquid *r/l* sounds, the whole thing landing as if on a pillow, "With a soft inland murmur." Violent language would not befit Wordsworth's purpose here, when the goal is only "powerful emotions recalled in tranquility," as he elsewhere describes the purpose of poetry. Hamlet's speech is declamatory, as befits the stage and the moment; Wordsworth's poem is reflective and introspective. Rhymes? Who needs them?

What we learn from blank verse, ultimately, is that rhyme is not poetry. It is an option, in English at least, although not in all other languages. Not only that, it was there first. The moment Old English gave way to that blend of Anglo-Saxon and Norman French that would become our language, rhymes found their way into our poetry. So while hearing someone say some variation of "It's not poetry if it doesn't rhyme" sets my teeth on edge, I do understand where that person got that idea. It isn't wrong to expect poems to ring the changes that rhyme makes possible; it isn't right to believe that those are the only poems in the language. Hey, with a vocabulary drawn from Germanic, French, Latin, Spanish, Gaelic, African, Indian, Persian, Arabic, and Native American roots, finding rhymes is just fun. And nearly limitless. Just stay away from "orange."

8

Look Who's Talking

─────────

I MIGHT AS WELL FESS UP RIGHT NOW: IT'S OUR FAULT. THAT WOULD be me and pretty much everybody else in the great fraternity-sorority of Persons Who Teach Poetry. We teachers led you to a terrible mistake through carelessness or sloppy thinking or simply not noticing. And we're sorry. The mistake? At some point, you will say or, worse, write the following about, say, Robert Frost's "The Road Not Taken":

"When Frost says, 'Two roads diverged, etc.'"

Why is that wrong? Because a poem is not a court deposition, a letter of recommendation, or a lover's note. Those are, we trust, true statements in the real world, reflecting someone's version of the God's honest truth about X or Y or Zed. If John writes to Marsha, "Meet me behind the school at 2:45," he darned well needs to back it up by showing up at the appointed moment and not sometime next week. A poem is not a true document but rather an imaginative utterance. And the imaginative part extends to the personage who utters it. When we assume that said personage is the Poet (as if that's his name, John Q. Poet), we run the risk of missing the point.

I know, students and others do this with fiction, too, speak of the author as the same as the narrator. But they know, even as they're saying that "Melville says, 'Call me Ishmael,'" that it isn't Melville, the author, but Ishmael, the character, who speaks. That "me" following "call" is a dead giveaway. The author is free to choose a narrator in the same way he chooses a character: he makes that narrator up. Will the narrative presence be harshly judgmental or gently amused about the characters' actions? Will it be aloof and godlike or chummy and welcoming? How will it sound? Will it even have an identifiable gender? So many decisions to make.

Yeah, but behind the narrator there's the author. We can rely on her.

You think so? Is the "author" we perceive behind the work the same as the author who sits down to a bowl of oatmeal every morning rather than a plate of eggs? Or is it, too, a fiction? Wayne C. Booth, in *The Rhetoric of Fiction* (1961), introduced the wonderfully useful term "implied author" to explain this questionable being. On the one hand, the implied author is a little like the Holy Ghost, perceived rather than seen directly. On the other, it might be better understood as an attitude, or maybe a set of attitudes, about the proceedings in the novel or story. What makes the term so useful is that it removes questions about "what the author really meant." We can infer what this phantasm "means" only by recourse to the text, and we can eliminate speculation as to the "real" author, who will for us always remain a little unreal and whose motives are always out of reach. It works in nonfiction as well.

This voice you've been reading is a creation I struggled with years ago when I wrote the first of these books. It makes use of many elements of my own personality (and not inevitably the best ones), but it foregrounds some and hides others. I spent months unlearning habits of academic writing, like diving into lengthy, detailed analyses (but not only that), that I had labored for years to master, while at the same time increasing certain silly parts of my being that I had previously stifled for the good of my career. And then I had to dial back the newly released goofy factor—some will say not enough—to try to reach a version of me that could seem welcoming, a little flippant, warm(ish), and yet just authoritative enough for the occasion. It's still a daily struggle. That "voice" is my nonfiction equivalent of a narrator; the set of decisions that underwrites is the implied author. And just for the record, I generally opt for cold breakfasts.

Thought I'd forgotten about poetry, didn't you? These decisions all take place there as well. And again, some decisions are obvious. When Robert Browning lets the evil, serial-wife-killing duke speak for himself in "My Last Duchess," we can tell that's not Browning, who loved his wife and was not a duke. Or when the mother tells her son, "Life for me ain't been no crystal stair" in "Mother to Son," we know that Langston Hughes is a man, so that can't be his true voice. When we discuss poems, we refer to *speakers* rather than narrators, since poems do not inevitably involve the telling of a story but almost always have someone say something. And many speakers are obviously characters, so they are easily discerned as having lives of their own.

What about the others? What about speakers who may well be some version of their creators? Here's where the enterprise gets murky. Let's take a fan favorite:

> Two roads diverged in a yellow wood,
> And sorry I could not travel both
> And be one traveler, long I stood
> And looked down one as far as I could
> To where it bent in the undergrowth;
>
> Then took the other, as just as fair,
> And having perhaps the better claim,
> Because it was grassy and wanted wear;
> Though as for that the passing there
> Had worn them really about the same,
>
> And both that morning equally lay
> In leaves no step had trodden black.

Oh, I kept the first for another day!
Yet knowing how way leads on to way,
I doubted if I should ever come back.

I shall be telling this with a sigh
Somewhere ages and ages hence:
Two roads diverged in a wood, and I—
I took the one less traveled by,
And that has made all the difference.

Let's do what we can to rescue this fine poem from commencement-ceremony purgatory. "The Road Not Taken" is a less stable poem and Robert Frost certainly a more dangerous poet than they are generally taken to be when the graduating class is being enjoined to turn away from the madding crowd and seek out new territories.

From the first moment, Frost builds the poem around the difficulty of choice. First, the two paths merely diverge from each other, with no further description. Already, however, the speaker is sorry that in choosing the one, he will close off the possibility of taking the other. Then the trouble begins. Studying the first path as far as he can, he elects the other, claiming it as "just as fair." But hold on: it may have "a better claim" because it "was grassy and wanted wear." And the moment we're glad that's settled, he reverses himself again, saying that traffic had worn them "about the same" and that on this particular morning, no travelers' steps had crushed the leaves underfoot to turn them black. Then he hedges his bet, saying that he "kept the first for another day," although in the time it takes the eye to traverse a line break he switches again, admitting that "I doubted if I should ever come back." Come on! Which is it? Was the path less worn or not? More inviting or less? Superior or inferior in any way?

Before tackling the resolution of this conundrum, I'm going to cheat a little here and introduce a fact about the real poet. Frost said that he was inspired to write this poem by his neighbor and friend from the time when he resided in England, Edward Thomas, also a poet of importance. Thomas could never, according to Frost, make up his mind when presented with two alternatives. Thomas's agonizing over every decision *can* be seen as inspiring the speaker's own challenges with decision making. Since, however, the vast majority of readers of this poem has been and will continue to be blithely unaware that such a person as Edward Thomas ever existed, we need not adduce him as a key factor. Still, he adds a small amount of pleasure to our reading. But doesn't change what comes next.

The garden-variety reading of the poem reduces the final stanza of the poem to its last two lines: "I took the road less traveled by / And that has made all the difference." In and of itself, this sentence is problematic: Was the road, based on what he's already told us, really less traveled; and what is meant by "all the difference"? It seems to me that the common version falls back on biographical material that simply doesn't apply, namely that Frost became honored and fêted, complete with honorary degrees and a Nobel Prize. Except that the Frost who wrote this poem, *when* he wrote the poem, was an unpublished poet trying to gather materials for a first book. He has no idea where he will be "ages and ages hence" when he tells his perfected version of this story.

The greater problem with such a reading is what it omits. That final stanza is a single sentence, and to skip its opening clause is to miss the point. "I shall be telling this with a sigh," the speaker says, "Somewhere ages and ages hence." In other words, the plan is to make a story out of this moment, whatever the outcome might prove to be. That "sigh" injects just the right degree of wistfulness. A sigh can signal resignation or regret or satisfaction or exhaustion, depending on the person and the circumstance. In this case, the ending being very much in doubt, it suggests something backward-looking, reminiscence if not nostalgia. What it does not signal is truth. What the speaker says is, "At some unknown time and in some as-yet-unforeseen place, I'm going to tell this story about myself. However things turn out, I will use this decision to explain the course of my journey." He doesn't even know if it will be true. But that's beside the point. What does matter is that he has been able to turn this small event into something larger, life-altering, even. If we choose to understand that he means that this choice made him a success, well, he can't stop us, but he doesn't have to approve. Rather the opposite.

Frost, you see, is a moralist. How else to explain this statement, "These poems are written in parable so the wrong people won't understand, and so get saved"? Really? Saved? Yes, that's what he said. Combine that with "parable" and "the wrong people" and he doesn't sound all that user-friendly. Nor is he. Almost all his most memorable lines don't say what those quoting them think they do. Consider his most famous, "Good fences make good neighbors." Yes, it closes "Mending Wall," but coming at the end doesn't mean Frost believes it. His speaker doesn't even believe it; he's quoting his neighbor, whom he has earlier compared to "an old-stone savage armed" and suggested is a man of limited intellect and vision, a man who "moves in darkness." He has, in short, been having fun at the neighbor's expense. Yet he has him repeat the line, as if it says all that needs saying. Holding that line as our takeaway from the poem is the very definition of not being saved. Yet the speaker may be a little smug himself, with his desire to say that it's elves that knock over the stones of the wall. For our purposes, we want to distinguish between on the one hand the speaker, who is also a character, and his neighbor, both of whom are imperfect stand-ins for the poet, and on the other this shadier figure, the implied author, who seems to have questions about both men. Read this way, the resolution of the poem is less clear-cut than it seems at first. True, we can largely dismiss the neighbor's viewpoint, but might there be more truth in it than the speaker is willing to concede? For that matter, to what degree is the speaker correct in his own views? There is a good deal of room for interpretation here. We do well to remember that there is always some daylight between the speaker of a poem and this ghostly stand-in, the implied author.

Okay, but what about poets who seem to enter their poems more personally and less in parable than Frost? That would include some of the Romantics, especially Wordsworth, as well as later incarnations of that tradition such as the Beats and the Confessional poets. Where, precisely, does someone like Sylvia Plath, who seems to so fully inhabit her verse, stand in relation to the things said? These poets and others like them are deeply autobiographical, in Plath's case *confessional*, and the filter, if any, is scarcely in evidence. Take a poem opening we've looked at before, Wordsworth's "Lines Composed a Few Miles above Tintern Abbey":

> *Five years have past; five summers, with the length*
> *Of five long winters! and again I hear*
> *These waters, rolling from their mountain-springs*
> *With a soft inland murmur.—Once again*
> *Do I behold these steep and lofty cliffs,*
> *That on a wild secluded scene impress*
> *Thoughts of more deep seclusion; and connect*
> *The landscape with the quiet of the sky.*

In contrast to Frost's poems, this one feels less *mediated* by any sort of filter, as if it pours not from his brain but from his heart. This stance is shared by several of Wordsworth's fellow Romantics (we have to exempt Lord Byron, adept at maintaining that distance): better to be thought artless than heartless. This aesthetic position is largely in reaction to the previous century or so, when poetry was all about brains and logic and wit. Wordsworth and Co. want it to be about emotions and full of soul, which goes a long way toward their worship of "the rustic" and "the child," two beings supposedly untouched by modernity and sophistication. Wordsworth is, after all, responsible for the line, "The Child is father of the Man," in his short poem "My Heart Leaps Up." Before that, let's look at "Tintern Abbey," with its emphasis on the five years that have passed since that prior trip and its celebration of the wildness, seclusion, and distance from human society of this stretch of river. Yet those opening lines give the lie to this poem as some sort of unmediated cri de coeur. The emotions he feels are genuine, make no mistake there, but they are far from the spontaneous upwelling he wishes to suggest. After all, he has had five years to consider those emotions, consider how best to express them. Not exactly "the spontaneous overflow of powerful feeling," as he has it elsewhere, but rather the second half of that line, "it takes its origin from emotion recollected in tranquility." That is not a flaw, nor does it suggest the poem is a failure or somehow "inauthentic," merely that this is a work of art and not a diary. After all, at the end of "The Heart Leaps Up," he says not that his days are bound each to each by natural piety, but "I could wish my days to be / Bound each to each by natural piety." There is a world of distance contained in that "could wish."

Much the same is true of the Confessional poets: Plath, Anne Sexton, Robert Lowell, W. D. Snodgrass, and John Berryman, among others. Yes, on one level, they are laying bare their hearts, and we feel ripped apart when Plath bleeds on the page in, say, "Daddy." At the same time, there is a great deal of fictionalizing going on in the poems of *Ariel*, as in those moment when she turns her father and her husband, Ted Hughes, into Nazis, black-clad, belted, and booted. We can only reject the distance between the living poet and the speaker (and implied author) by concluding that these poems are not art but the product of madness, a record only of fevered dreams, an assumption that seriously diminishes the greatness of the poetry. Speaking of dreams, Berryman goes even further, insinuating a character named "Henry" into his *Dream Songs*. First readers of *77 Dream Songs* were inclined to identify Henry as Berryman, a conclusion that he explicitly rejected in the preface to the subsequent collection. So there is always at least a tiny bit of distance between the artist and the poem.

How much? Ah, there's the nub of the matter. The issue here is irony. That distance between the poet and the animating intelligence of her work is a form of irony. Frost has that in abundance; Wordsworth not so much. But that doesn't mean that Wordsworth or Plath are without irony, only that they have a lower tolerance for it, which I think explains why Wordsworth and his pals rejected the seventeenth-century Metaphysical poets (think John Donne and Andrew Marvell), whose work was shot through with wit and intellect and irony, just as it explains why those earlier poets made a comeback in the age of Eliot and Stevens and, yes, even Frost. What we mean by irony here is that gap between what a poet knows or thinks and what he or she allows the poem to say. Some will foreground that gap while others will hide it deep. No matter how deeply buried it is, though, it remains always present. Sometimes we just have to look a little harder. And listen carefully to that speaker. The poet's voice is a powerful instrument, but much more powerful is the poem's voice.

9

If It's Square, It's a Sonnet

WHENEVER I WOULD ASK MY CLASS WHAT FORM A PARTICULAR poem employed, the answer was always the same: sonnet. Why? Because it is the only lyric form I had any hope that they might know. Or need to. Is the quality of your life harmed by not recognizing on sight something like the rondeau? That's what I thought. The other reason is that no other poem is so versatile, so ubiquitous, so various, so blessedly short as the sonnet.

So after I told them that first time that it's a sonnet, and half of them groaned in belated recognition and the others asked how I knew that so fast, I told them that I counted the lines when I noticed the geometry of the poem. What's that? they would ask. Well, I responded, trying to milk the moment for suspense, it's square. The miracle of the sonnet, you see, is that it is fourteen lines long and written almost always in iambic pentameter. And ten syllables of English are about as long as fourteen lines are high. See? Square.

My guess is that if you locked ten students in a room with an unfamiliar sonnet and asked them, "What's the first thing you notice about this poem?" you'd get maybe one of them, after a number of minutes, who would write down, "It's a sonnet, wise guy. Now let me out." The others would tell you something substantive about what the poem actually says. Not a bad thing, but it misses a key starting point for reading the poem. On the other hand, if you locked ten professors of literature in a room with that same sonnet, the time frame would be seconds, no more than thirty at that, and they'd all say, "It's a sonnet." Or nine of them would, but the postmodernist would be deconstructing the experience. Now this would be hard to prove, since no sane person would want to be locked in a room with ten professors of literature for as long as thirty seconds, even with a sonnet. But I figure that's what would happen.

Okay, great, so I can identify one type of poem, you say. *Who cares?* Many of my students actually asked that, while many more were too polite but clearly thought it. And the answer is, the reader of said sonnet should care. I think people who read poems for enjoyment should always read the poem first, without a formal or stylistic care in the world. They should not begin by counting lines, or looking at line endings to find the rhyme scheme, if any. I also think people should read novels without peeking at the ending. Other people, that is. I want them to do that because I want them to really enjoy the poem or novel. I, on the other hand, routinely violate both of those pleasure principles. But after you've had your first pleasure, one of the additional pleasures is seeing how the poet worked that magic on you. And at least some part of the answer, if that magic came in a sonnet, is *form*.

You might suppose that a poem that is only fourteen lines long is only capable of doing one thing. And you'd be right. It can't have epic scope, it can't undertake subplots, it can't carry much narrative water. But you'd also be wrong. It can do two things. And it probably does. The sonnet has been a big part of English poetry since the 1500s, and there are a few major types of sonnet, with myriad variations. But what most of them will do is have two parts, one of eight lines and one of six lines. A Petrarchan sonnet uses a rhyme scheme that ties the first eight lines (the octave) together, followed by a rhyme scheme that unifies the last six (sestet). A Shakespearean sonnet, on the other hand, tends to divide up by four: the first four lines, the next four, the third four, and the last four, which turn out to be only two. But even here, the first two groups of four (which even I know adds up to eight) have some unity of statement, as do the last six, which break down as four and two. Shakespeare himself often works a statement all its own into that last couplet, but it also usually ties in pretty closely with the third quatrain. All these technical terms, and it's not even physics; still, who can say that a poem isn't engineered? A sonnet, then, we might think of as having two units of meaning, closely related to be sure, with a shift of some sort taking place between them. Sometimes, and especially in the modern and postmodern period, those units slip and slide a little, and the octave doesn't quite contain its meaning, which slides onto the ninth line. Still, the basic pattern is 8/6. Let's look at a poem. Even better, a sonnet.

How about Christina Rossetti's "An Echo from Willow-Wood":

> Two gazed into a pool, he gazed and she,
>   Not hand in hand, yet heart in heart, I think,
>   Pale and reluctant on the water's brink,
> As on the brink of parting which must be,
>   Each eyed the other's aspect, she and he,
>   Each felt one hungering heart leap up and sink,
>   Each tasted bitterness which both must drink,
> There on the brink of life's dividing sea.
> Lilies upon the surface, deep below
>   Two wistful faces craving each for each,
>   Resolute and reluctant without speech:—
> A sudden ripple made the faces flow,
>   One moment joined, to vanish out of reach:
>   So those heart joined, and ah! were parted so.
> (ca. 1870)

I picked this poem for three reasons. First, it's out of copyright (and never underestimate the cheapness of humanities professors). Second, it has neither a "thee" nor a "thou" in sight, not an "e'er" nor an "o'er," so we eliminate some of that ball of confusion that older poetry slings at hapless modern readers. And third, I like Christina Rossetti, probably because I never had to study her, and I think more people should read and like her.

But on with the poem. I can hear the geometrically inclined out there saying, "Hey, it's not really square." True, but it's approximately square, and that's how the eye will initially perceive it. So the first question (no peeking): How many sentences? I loved to ask my poetry students that question. They generally were so buffaloed by all those separate lines, they didn't notice that the words actually make sentences. The answer is two, as you already know, since you peeked. Second question, can you guess where the first period falls?

Right. End of line eight. The guy in the back of the class with his cap on backwards thinks I cheated and picked out a poem that made my point. Would I cheat? Well, yes, I might, but in this case I didn't. Didn't have to. I plunked open my trusty Victorian poetry anthology, picked the first Christina Rossetti sonnet without a "thee" in it, and this is the one.

So, the octave is a single unit of meaning. And what is the most basic unit of meaning in a poem? The line? The octave? Nope. If the poem is any good, its basic unit of meaning is the sentence. Just like all other writing. That's why if you stop at the end of every line, a poem makes no sense. It's not written in lines, but in sentences. What Rossetti does here is construct her sentences, which have to carry her meaning, so that they work within the form she has chosen, which is the sonnet. Her rhyme scheme proves to be a little idiosyncratic, since she elects to repeat the same rhymes in both quatrains of the octave: ABBAABBA. Then she picks an equally uncommon rhyme scheme for the sestet: CDDCDC. Still, in each case, the particular pattern reinforces a basic concept—these eight lines carry one idea; those six another, related idea.

And this is why form matters, and why professors pay attention to form: it just might mean something. Will every sonnet consist of only two sentences? No, that would be boring. Will they all employ this rhyme scheme? No, and they may not even have rhyme schemes, as we have seen. But when a poet chooses to write a sonnet, rather than, say, *Paradise Lost*, it's not because he's lazy. One of those old French thinkers, Blaise Pascal, I think, apologized for writing such a long letter, saying, "I had not time to write a short one." Sonnets are like that, short poems that take far more time, because everything has to be perfect, than long ones.

We owe it to poets, I think, to notice that they've gone to this trouble, and to ourselves, to understand the nature of the thing we're reading. When you start to read a poem, then, look at the shape.

ALTERNATIVE APPROACHES TO RHYME

SO IS EVERY sonnet written in one of two basic forms? Must the sonnet world divide into Petrarchan and Shakespearean? We recently saw one by Frost in terza rima, admittedly a rarity, and it introduces some unusual problems. Most poems with this rhyme scheme sit on the page in three-line stanzas, with the middle line of each stanza giving the rhyme for the first and third lines of the next. *Big deal*, you say, *why does that matter here?* It's actually a very good question, and kind of a big deal. The answer is math. You know that bit about octaves and sestets? An eight-line section is not divisible by a three-line pattern, or not in any way that avoids bloodshed. But to end the statement or set of statements on line eight will mean that the idea level of the poem will be at war with the rhyme scheme. Again with the bloodshed! Moreover, the math works against the rhyme scheme running all the way through the poem (three into fourteen equals ugly), so we know that the poem must end with a couplet, and those usually form their own concluding thought. That means that ending the first movement after line nine leaves a three-line group and a couplet. Maybe, but don't expect readers to thank you.

Okay, wise guy, what do you recommend?

I recommend nothing, except that we look at what Frost and, in another context, Shelley does with the form. What we see in this poem is essentially a single movement of thought, a sort of list of the ways in which the speaker has been acquainted with the night. That movement actually concludes with line thirteen, when the clock "Proclaimed the time was neither wrong nor right." The fourteenth, then, is merely a restatement of line one.

This notion of a sonnet whose alternate rhyme scheme changes the structure of the poem carries over into the realm of those unrhymed sonnets I mentioned a moment ago. Yes, there are such things, and mostly they are modern developments. And some still adhere to the old rules. W. H. Auden is sometimes credited with the first unrhymed, or *blank*, sonnet in English, "The Secret Agent" (1928), which in every respect other than being blank verse is perfectly regular—iambic pentameter, an eight-and-six-line organization, and so on. On the other hand, W. S. Merwin's later sonnets generally display a single movement of thought or, if doubled, a movement that does not break after line eight. His "Morning near the End of May" can be read as containing a slight shift in what would otherwise be the sestet, while others such as "The Handwriting of the Old" or "Breakfast Cup" (all 2016) clearly do not, as statements begun in line eight or earlier carry over to line nine. Well, why not? Poetic practice isn't the Laws of Soccer. In general, we cannot predict what structure blank verse sonnets may take, but they may veer away from the conventional.

So, too, with half-rhyme sonnets. Those would be sonnets with a rhyme scheme but where the "rhymes" may be something short of perfect. They are also known as slant rhymes, and some can get pretty slanted. In his sonnet sequences "Lachrimae" and "An Apology for the Revival of Christian Architecture in England" (both 1978), Geoffrey Hill rhymes "pentecosts" with "quests," "hell" with "avail," "name" with "condemn," and "hood" with "servitude." All imperfect but completely permissible. The resulting sonnets are otherwise quite regular, although he does break the sestets up into two triplets. In his sequence "Clearances," Seamus Heaney is equally free with his rhyming "line" with "linen" in one case (a near rhyme for the eye rather than the ear) and "Holy Week" with "candlestick" in another, a definite stretch. This cavalier approach carries over, somewhat, into the question of structure as well. While this sonnet (number six of eight) maintains the eight-and-six formula and the first three sonnets actually display the break with extra spacing, the remaining four mark the turn not after line eight but in the middle or at the end of line seven. This one shifts content direction at the midpoint, while it finishes the rhyme of "cross-wind" with the half-rhyme of "hand to hand," offers the self-rhyme "happened" in lines nine and ten, giving the poem a slightly strange rhyme scheme: ABABCDCDEEFGFG. Okay, then, we can safely say that half-rhymed or unrhymed sonnets do not *cause* structural change, at least not in the way that use of terza rima seems to, based on an extremely small sample. On the other hand, they may go hand in hand with a sense of experimentation that may lead to rejection of the 8/6 structural pattern. That makes sense, given that the traditional rhyme schemes encourage adherence to the conventional pattern. What we learn here is the thing we've known all along, that writers are people, and where people are concerned, there's no predicting what they may do.

OCCASIONS FOR WHIMSY

MOSTLY, WE'VE BEEN talking about poems that take the form seriously. But the sonnet also invites fun, and even fun at the form's expense. Here is American poet Billy Collins's "Sonnet," which may be the best-known sonnet of our time:

> *All we need is fourteen lines, well, thirteen now,*
> *and after this one just a dozen*
> *to launch a little ship on love's storm-tossed seas,*
> *then only ten more left like rows of beans.*
> *How easily it goes unless you get Elizabethan*

and insist the iambic bongos must be played
and rhymes positioned at the ends of lines,
one for every station of the cross.
But hang on here while we make the turn
into the final six where all will be resolved,
where longing and heartache will find an end,
where Laura will tell Petrarch to put down his pen,
take off those crazy medieval tights,
blow out the lights, and come at last to bed.

This particular model takes a lot of liberties with the form, including jettisoning rhyme, varying line length and meter, and making the form itself the subject of the poem. That seems pretty disrespectful, doesn't it? At the same time, it is the best explanation of that form you will ever read. Besides, the disrespect is playful in a way that reminds us that the form itself is a type of play. Playful and instructive—what a concept!

What Collins does here is use the form to discuss and demonstrate how it works, while at the same time embedding a typical subject. The first time or two he counts down the lines left—something most young people assigned to write a sonnet have done, usually the night before it's due—it merely seems like a stunt. Saying "All we need is fourteen lines, well thirteen now," that line being finished, may be cute but doesn't augur well for a poem of substance to ensue. But even as he counts down, he introduces the notion that the first eight lines establish a topic, even as he hints at an eventual theme of love. So when at line nine he says that "we make the turn" toward resolution, he explains how a sonnet is traditionally structured while leading us toward that resolution. Having been so irreverent early in the poem toward the idea of sonnets, he brings us back to its founding father (Petrarch was not the inventor but was certainly the first truly great sonneteer) and his constant subject, his beloved Laura, calling him back to bed. Let's credit Collins with generosity in giving Petrarch the consummation he never achieved in life; Laura and the poet may or may not ever have conversed, much less cohabited, and the resulting sonnets are entirely taken up with longing and romantic anguish rather than fulfillment. Along the way, Collins has great fun in dismissing rhyme as a quasi-religious exercise ("the stations of the cross") and rejecting the metrical regularity he describes as "iambic bongos," something of an improvement on Heaney's "iambic drums" from a couple of decades earlier. As with much of Collins's work, his impulse toward parody unmasks sometimes-unconsidered possibilities in the form.

Oh, and one more thing. Having brought us up to the present day, this discussion can't be complete without a nod toward a Certain Party:

Sonnet 73

> *That time of year thou may'st in me behold*
> *When yellow leaves, or none, or few, do hang*
> *Upon those boughs which shake against the cold,*
> *Bare ruin'd choirs, where late the sweet birds sang.*
> *In me thou see'st the twilight of such day,*
> *As after sunset fadeth in the west,*
> *Which by and by black night doth take away,*
> *Death's second self, that seals up all in rest.*
> *In me thou see'st the glowing of such fire*
> *That on the ashes of his youth doth lie,*
> *As the death-bed whereon it must expire*
> *Consum'd with that which it was nourish'd by.*
> *This thou perceivest, which makes thy love more strong,*
> *To love that well which thou must leave ere long.*

Oh, like you were getting out of here without a sonnet by HIM! This structure is called Shakespearean, for crying out loud. And what makes it so? A very English turn of mind. It's as if the Elizabethans, or one at least, looked at the Italian model and had two thoughts. The

first was, What an elegant form. And the second, How can we sim-
plify it? Essentially, the Petrarchan sonnet involves two clear move-
ments. The octave is composed of two four-line sections, or quatrains,
that rhyme either ABABCDCD or ABBACDDC and then a more intri-
cately rhymed sestet, usually DEFDEF. But maybe it could simply be
three quatrains and a closing couplet. The idea organization is still
the same: one movement in the first eight lines, another in the sestet.
So generally the same. But the quatrain-and-couplet arrangement in
those final six lines permits a new wrinkle. Lines nine through twelve
form their own statement that is self-contained, and then the final two
constitute a conclusion. And when we're talking about loving life all
the more because the awareness of death is a full-time reality, there is
nothing more conclusive than that.

The imagery in the octave is uniformly autumnal—seasonal,
psychological, spiritual, physical. He gives us fallen leaves, ruined
churches, harsh winds, twilight and the coming of night. It may not
be winter yet, but that's close upon us. He ends that movement with
sleep, which in Elizabethan thinking was merely the poor cousin of
death. The third quatrain continues and completes that movement by
making it personal: "I am like the fire that has burnt itself nearly out,"
he says, invoking "death-bed" in place of hearth, and then providing
the brilliant concept of the fire as being consumed by that which once
nourished it. The final two lines provide a sort of coda, suggesting
how the prospect of leaving this life makes it all the more dear. That
sense of longing becoming more acute as the thing longed for—life, in
this case—begins to slip away has never been better expressed.

This poem will grow on you. Or maybe you'll grow into it. I
recommend learning to love it while you're young; that way, it will
become more and more yours as you move closer to the age of the
speaker. What a concept: a sonnet about not love and romance but
aging and death. Maybe Billy Collins didn't know about this.

10

A Haiku, a Rondeau, and a Villanelle Walk into a Bar

Sometimes, if I want to see blank faces, I will mention the word "sestina." There are a lot of tricks in the book, but this one is special. It never fails. This is not an indictment of students, current culture, or the state of the American education system. Unless you are a poet of a certain type or a scholar of poetry at a fairly high level, there is simply no reason to know the term. Even with a hundred billion neurons in the brain, some things aren't worth the storage space.

SHORT STUFF

I know, I know. You hear "poetic forms" and your skin starts to crawl. But let's start with a couple of forms that should never scare anyone. Most of us encountered the *haiku* in the middle grades, which is about right. At that age, we can count and mostly manage simple sentences, which is all that's required. The rules as we know them: three lines, 5–7–5 syllables respectively, two images juxtaposed. A friend of mine has long claimed that the last line of all haiku should be "cherry blossoms," but that's just silly. Only four syllables.

On one level, the haiku is simplicity itself. The form is a little more complex in Japanese, but not greatly so. Here's one from Basho, the seventeenth-century godfather of the haiku:

> An old silent pond . . .
> A frog jumps into the pond,
> splash! Silence again.

Simple, right? You read a good haiku and think, I could do that. And you probably could. But it's not the form that's tough; it's the compression. What can you say in so small a space, and how well can you say it? There is structure, but a haiku isn't a house, it's a crystal.

That crystalline quality was one reason the haiku found favor in the early twentieth century with the rise of Imagism, a movement built around stripping poetry down to its most basic element, the creation of a brilliant image. Think Pound's Metro station and Williams's red wheelbarrow. Those aren't haiku, but they are tiny, single-focused, and wonderfully evocative. What's not to love?

So what about everybody's favorite tiny poem, the limerick? Yes, Virginia, it is a real poetic form. Only the poems are not so serious. We're talking a five-line poem rhyming AABBA. The meter is generally mixed, iambic and anapestic, meaning two unstressed syllables followed by one stressed. Every line begins with an iamb or sometimes a trochee, and lines one, two, and five then have two of those anapestic feet ("da-DUM da-da-DUM da-da-DUM"), lines two and four just one ("da-DUM da-da-DUM"). It seems to be a form that says, "Insert joke here":

> There was an Old Man with a beard,
> Who said, "It is just as I feared!—
> Two Owls and a Hen,
> Four Larks and a Wren,
> Have all built their nests in my beard."

Those two short lines are almost custom designed—in the form, not just in this poem—for the delivery of a punch line. Edward Lear is fond of reusing one of the rhyming words from the first two lines to end the poem, a tendency not widely shared. He is also a writer of clean limericks, another trait that is observed somewhat less than universally. Some commentators, among them George Bernard Shaw, claim that a poem is only a limerick if it observes the rules *and* is dirty. Most people, by the time they reach their majority, will have heard at least a couple dirty limericks. Rugby players, hundreds. There is even a limerick to that effect from the well-known poet Anonymous:

> *The limerick packs laughs anatomical*
> *Into space that is quite economical.*
> *But the good ones I've seen*
> *So seldom are clean*
> *And the clean ones so seldom are comical.*

You can't say fairer than that.

VILLANELLE

A VILLANELLE LOOKS as if it has nineteen lines, but it really only has thirteen, since two of them get repeated. Repeatedly. Lines one and three of the first stanza form the refrain and then are deployed alternately. This means that line one is the refrain of stanzas two and four, while line two is the refrain of stanzas three and five. They then come together at the end, standing as the final two lines of the poem. Again with the math! Maybe it's not poetry people dislike but counting. It's far easier to see than to envision, so let's look at Dylan Thomas's most famous poem, whose title is also its first line:

> *Do not go gentle into that good night,*
> *Old age should burn and rave at close of day;*
> *Rage, rage against the dying of the light.*

Though wise men at their end know dark is right,
Because their words had forked no lightning they
Do not go gentle into that good night.

Good men, the last wave by, crying how bright
Their frail deeds might have danced in a green bay,
Rage, rage against the dying of the light.

Wild men who caught and sang the sun in flight,
And learn, too late, they grieved it on its way,
Do not go gentle into that good night.

Grave men, near death, who see with blinding sight
Blind eyes could blaze like meteors and be gay,
Rage, rage against the dying of the light.

And you, my father, there on the sad height,
Curse, bless, me now with your fierce tears, I pray.
Do not go gentle into that good night.
Rage, rage against the dying of the light.

The beauty is that, however confusing the form is in the abstract, there is nothing hard about a good one in practice, and this is a not-merely-good one. Here is another use of terza rima in poetry: the rhyme scheme is merely ABA for each stanza with an added line (for an ABAA scheme) on the last one. It has a specialized form, of course, because of the repeated lines. I tried typing it out, but the word processor had ideas of its own and the schematic rendering just made things worse. But you have only to look at the poem again to see how smoothly it reads in practice. As with every form, the villanelle's rules make for some specialized outcomes. For one thing, you have to plan for every stanza to form a complete thought, usually in two lines with the refrain acting as, well, a refrain. Notice that Thomas's second lines are end-stopped with at least a comma, except for the second, where "Because their words had forked no lightning they" requires "Do not go gentle into that good night" to make any sense. Only the final stanza comes to a full stop after line two; lesser punctuation marks off the other four. On one level, that's a lot of pressure, the need to make every stanza a complete statement. On the other, the poet knows in advance what his third line will be, so he can build toward it. That's the challenge of the form. It also carries a major reward: because of the repetition of both refrain lines at the end, no form feels more satisfyingly finished than the villanelle. It more or less says, "There! Wasn't that grand?" And in this case, it certainly is.

There is one further benefit, compositionally, to the villanelle. True, the form has very strict regulations for the number of lines and how they are arrayed, but it has no such restrictions on meter. I'm pretty sure this was an oversight by some committee, but it offers a bit of freedom to the poet. Most nineteenth-century villanelles in English were in tetrameter or even trimeter, while the majority of twentieth-century versions were in pentameter. The one thing that all seem to agree on is that, having chosen a meter, the poet is obliged to stick with it.

SESTINA

I'M GOING TO let one of us off the hook here with just a warning. I said before that there is almost no occasion for civilians to know this form, and I'm sticking with it. The *sestina* originated around 1200 with one of the troubadours, Arnaut Daniel, whom Dante called "*il miglior fabbro*" ("the better maker") but still consigned to Purgatory. The form is devilish in its own right. The poem consists of six six-line stanzas, often with a three-line epilogue, called an *envoi*, appended at the end. There is typically no rhyming (French, remember?), but the last words of all six lines of the first stanza are also the last words of the lines of each subsequent stanza, with a kind of round-robin change of order. The sixth rhyme hustles up to the front of the line: 123456, 612345,

561234, and so on. The form is rather uncommon in English. Edmund Spenser has one and Sir Philip Sidney three in the sixteenth century, and Ezra Pound has a famous one in the twentieth century, and there are a few scattered others, chiefly from a period of Francophile poetic practice in the late nineteenth century. On the whole, however, you're pretty safe from sestina attack. Actually, I'm thinking it may be the sestina form and not lust that led Dante to make Daniel do penance in Purgatory.

RONDEAU AND TRIOLET

Sonnets, of course, we have discussed elsewhere, but there's an odd cousin, a sort of almost-sonnet, that came out of medieval France and made its way in a slightly updated form to sixteenth-century England and is called a *rondeau*. Even if we don't know its history, we know that pretty much whenever we find an *e* and an *a* hanging out with a *u* (think "beauty"), the French are implicated. And if we had any doubts, it employs the word "rentrement," which can only come from one spot on earth. The rondeau consists of fifteen lines divided unevenly among three stanzas, with only two rhymes and a repeat of the first phrase of the first line, which is the rentrement. The rhyme scheme, as you may have surmised, is peculiar: AABBA-AABR-AABBAR, where R indicates rentrement, that repeated first phrase.

You might suppose that with this lengthy pedigree and exotic rules, including how to make a plural, that rondeaux (see?) would be the exclusive property of mighty fancy poets. Not so. Some of the most famous examples come from very plainspoken men, including Paul Laurence Dunbar and the following man.

If Canadians—and plenty of Americans and British subjects, too—wear poppies in their lapels on November 11, it is because of this 1915 poem. Its author, Major John McCrae, a doctor with the Canadian Expeditionary Force in World War I, wrote it in response to the death of a close comrade. Poppies, he knew, are among the first colonizers of disturbed ground.

In Flanders Fields

In Flanders fields the poppies blow
Between the crosses, row on row,
That mark our place; and in the sky,
The larks, still bravely singing, fly,
Scarce heard amid the guns below.

We are the dead; short days ago
We lived, felt dawn, saw sunset glow,
Loved and were loved, and now we lie
In Flanders fields.

Take up our quarrel with the foe!
To you from failing hands we throw
The torch; be yours to hold it high!
If ye break faith with us who die
We shall not sleep, though poppies grow
In Flanders fields.

This poem makes use of a three-part structure about as well as a poem possibly can. The first stanza contrasts growing poppies and singing larks with the stillness of cemeteries and the din of war. The second stanza identifies the speakers (and it is plural: "We are the dead") as the very recently dead in that war, while the third exhorts the living to keep faith with those who have sacrificed themselves, to take up the cause to which lives have been freely given. It also comes with a warning: "We shall not sleep" should the living shirk their duty; the poppies will provide no solace. The movement of the poem is sure and swift, as it must be, given the length.

The form makes demands of the poet, requiring him or her to be efficient, to fit thoughts into the available space and to order those thoughts in a way that makes sense within that space. It won't do, for instance, to carry over a thought to the next stanza and then begin a new thought midway through. At the same time, those thoughts, or rather the words that embody those thoughts, have to fit a very demanding framework of rhyme. The poet has only two rhyming sounds with which to work, and one recurs eight times, the other five. McCrae chooses wisely with the long *i* and long *o*, which give him as many options as one could reasonably desire. Each stanza has its own peculiarities regarding rhyme. In stanza one, the A rhyme finishes lines 1, 2, and 5, the B rhyme 3 and 4. Stanza two subtracts one rhyme from each sound, the A rhyme finishing lines 1 and 2, the B rhyme only line 3, followed by the half-line rentrement that rhymes only with itself. It is unusual in the extreme to see a rhyme occur only once in a stanza, but that is the requirement of this form. The third stanza, although it reprises the 1–2–5/3–4 scheme of the first, then appends the unrhymed rentrement to close the poem.

Perhaps the best feature of his rhyme scheme is that he withholds the key words "die" and "grow" until the last iteration of the respective rhymes. Clearly, the entire poem has been leading to the mention of dying, but he manages to keep the word itself at bay for as long as possible. We might expect the poppies in line one to "grow," but in fact they "blow," reserving the former word for the key location at the end.

McCrae, as fortune would have it, died of pneumonia in January 1918 and joined the host of the fallen at Wimereux Cemetery near Boulogne. A memorial was later erected in the vicinity of Ypres, near where he was operating on the wounded when he wrote the poem.

The rondeau is especially well suited to terse, three-part movements. Not large in scale, it permits, even requires, the quick transitions from point to point so that the meaning is not lost. And as this example demonstrates, it is capable of great thematic power.

A CLOSE COUSIN OF THE RONDEAU IS THE *TRIOLET*, ALSO FROM MEDI-eval France, also using repeated lines. The triolet is a mere eight lines with the wording of line one repeated in lines four and seven, while the wording of line two recurs in the last line. Changes in punctuation, as with many of these forms, is not merely permitted but almost mandatory. Thomas Hardy, one of the great English poets, shows just what can be done with changes in tiny marks between words in his "Birds at Winter Nightfall":

> *Around the house the flakes fly faster,*
> *And all the berries now are gone*
> *From holly and cotoneaster*
> *Around the house. The flakes fly!—faster*
> *Shutting indoors the crumb-outcaster*
> *We used to see upon the lawn*
> *Around the house. The flakes fly faster*
> *And all the berries now are gone!*

Notice how the lines change between "Around the house the flakes fly faster," "Around the house. The flakes fly!—faster," and "Around the house. The flakes fly faster." Clearly, Hardy was having a really good time wringing different meanings from those seven words by small shifts in punctuation. I have nothing concrete to go on but suspect he would have been most proud of the second half of the line in the last two. Strictly speaking, the exclamation mark in line eight is a violation of the strict repetition in the original form. That's okay, though: we generally value innovation more than convention. The form, after a brief vogue in the late nineteenth century, has largely fallen into disuse. That just means it is due for a reboot. After all, it is brief and a lot of fun.

ELEGY

An *ELEGY* is a poem memorializing someone recently deceased and, usually, known to the poet. Sometimes, as with Whitman's elegy for the fallen President Lincoln, "known to the poet" is a loose term:

> O Captain! my Captain! our fearful trip is done,
> The ship has weather'd every rack, the prize we sought
>   is won,
> The port is near, the bells I hear, the people all exulting,
> While follow eyes the steady keel, the vessel grim and
>   daring;
>   But O heart! heart! heart!
>   O the bleeding drops of red,
>   Where on the deck my Captain lies,
>   Fallen cold and dead.
>
> O Captain! my Captain! rise up and hear the bells;
> Rise up—for you the flag is flung—for you the bugle
>   trills,
> For you bouquets and ribbon'd wreaths—for you the
>   shores a-crowding,
> For you they call, the swaying mass, their eager faces
>   turning;
>   Here Captain! dear father!
>   This arm beneath your head!
>   It is some dream that on the deck,
>   You've fallen cold and dead.
>
> My Captain does not answer, his lips are pale and still,
> My father does not feel my arm, he has no pulse nor will,
> The ship is anchor'd safe and sound, its voyage closed
>   and done,

> From fearful trip the victor ship comes in with object
> won;
> > Exult O shores, and ring O bells!
> > But I with mournful tread,
> > Walk the deck my Captain lies,
> > Fallen cold and dead.

The thing about elegies is that they are a type rather than a form. An elegy can be pastoral, replete with shepherds overseeing invisible flocks and muses in fancy dress as shepherdesses. Or they can be Pindaric odes with three-part structures, a form Seamus Heaney employed in several elegies for victims of the Northern Irish troubles, as did Auden in his memorial poem for W. B. Yeats. Here, Whitman does something appropriate to the seagoing nineteenth century and makes Lincoln the fallen captain of a ship that he has brought safely home. In doing so, he allows full play to the irony that the president was killed just at the moment of triumph for him and the Republic. The contrast between exultation (which he emphasizes repeatedly) and mourning is played for maximum force. Notice that he uses his own three-part structure. In the first stanza, he emphasizes the success of the voyage—the prosecution of the war—which he follows in the second with an injunction to "My Captain" to rise up and hear the celebratory bells. In the final stanza, the harsh reality—already established with "You've fallen cold and dead" earlier—sets in: the Captain lies "pale and still," unable to witness the fruits of his labor. This is one of the most nearly perfect elegies ever written. Whitman could be a little lax about form elsewhere; in this case, he practices a rigorous discipline appropriate to his poem's occasion. If elegies hadn't already existed, this would be the model. Perhaps it is anyhow.

ODE

IN CONTRAST TO elegies, *odes* are characterized by form; in contrast to sonnets, that form is pretty loose. The typical definitions speak of somewhat greater length, seriousness of tone and subject, formal structure, and movement of mind. Pindar is the father of one type of ode, quite formal in language and possessing a three-part movement drawn from Greek dramatic choral odes. The first movement is called the *strophe*, which sets the poem in motion in a particular direction. The second, the *antistrophe*, offers a countermovement of thought. The third, or *epode*, attempts some sort of resolution between the warring elements of the first two. With the odes in Greek drama, the chorus actually moved in space to support the movement between thought and counterthought; the resolving epode did not always make an appearance in choral odes, depending on the demands of the dramatic action itself and the lack of resolution within the chorus, which represented the mind of the citizens of the locale where the play was set. Pindar, having no such limitations, pretty much always arrives at a conclusion. The odes of Horace were somewhat less formally strict and more meditative in tone and mood. Poets ever since have been choosing between Pindaric and Horatian approaches, although succeeding ages took liberties with the form. When the ode arrived in England, poets wrought their own changes until the form landed in the hands of John Keats, who employs as many stanzas as he deems necessary and wrote what are called the "Five Great Odes"—"Ode on a Grecian Urn," "Ode to a Nightingale," "Ode on Melancholy," "Ode to Psyche," and "To Autumn"—in 1819. A single year! After Keats, few poets in English undertook writing odes, as if they could see no way of measuring up, or perhaps he had done everything worth doing with the form. In "Ode on a Grecian Urn," Keats describes the urn in great detail, with a "sylvan" scene of a maiden being pursued by a would-be lover, the whole thing being caught in midchase, never to move forward. While another poet might lament the uncompleted action, Keats celebrates the perfection of the frozen moment.

Across the five stanzas of the poem, his thoughts develop and shift sinuously. He begins with an address to his subject:

Thou still unravish'd bride of quietness,
Thou foster-child of silence and slow time,
Sylvan historian, who canst thus express
A flowery tale more sweetly than our rhyme[.]

Like the fleeing maiden we've yet to meet, the urn is a "still unravish'd bride" not of some masculine figure but of "quietness." Or, if you prefer, it is a "foster-child of silence and slow time," not inevitable figures of parenthood. He salutes the urn as the superior storyteller who can "express / A flowery tale more sweetly than our rhyme." In the second stanza he elaborates on the theme of silence:

Heard melodies are sweet, but those unheard
Are sweeter; therefore, ye soft pipes, play on;
Not to the sensual ear, but, more endear'd,
Pipe to the spirit ditties of no tone[.]

This is music for the spirit rather than the ear. The beauty of the scene lies not in its realization but in its potentiality, for the way that it adumbrates its story rather than filling in all the details. Which praise he delivers in considerable detail. Throughout the second and third stanzas he lauds the permanence of the scene: the lover cannot extract his kiss, but on the other hand, neither he nor his quarry will ever age, nor will they be subject to the heartaches of real human love. Stanza four offers further detail of the urn's pictorial tale: priests coming to a sacrifice, leading a garlanded heifer, townsfolk following along and leaving, thereby, a town forever abandoned (because they are on the urn and not back at home), everything captured in clay. Forever.

He concludes the poem by praising the urn's permanence, against which contrasts the sad transience of real life, including his own art:

When old age shall this generation waste,
Thou shalt remain, in midst of other woe

Than ours, a friend to man, to whom thou say'st,
  "Beauty is truth, truth beauty,—that is all
    Ye know on earth, and all ye need to know."

"You'll be here long after my time has passed and some other genera-
tion has brought along its own miseries," he says. And then he gives to
the urn an aesthetic statement like no other, that not only are beauty
and truth the same thing, but that is all humans know or need to
know. Pretty bold stuff for a piece of crockery. The movement of the
poem from quiet admiration to audacious address is managed by a
series of small steps that belie its large ambitions.

This sort of poem, which strives to capture an object or scene or,
as here, a work of art, is called *ekphrastic*, which means something
like capturing other arts in words or translating from one medium to
another. Yet another literary term with which to astonish your friends
and confound your enemies. A very nice poem with which to contrast
this one is contemporary poet Eavan Boland's "The Photograph on
My Father's Desk," in which a set of actions—a woman placing her
hand on her throat in surprise, a pitcher of lemonade being stirred, a
man striding down a path—are similarly frozen by the act of photog-
raphy. Here, however, Boland emphasizes the incompleteness of the
action: each imminent action will never be fulfilled. Understanding
that she can never see beyond the surface of the picture, can never
achieve a fuller understanding of the scene, she displays more regret
than Keats at the action remaining static. Ekphrastic poems usually
seek to emulate the thing described in some way. Keats, for instance,
hopes for a similar kind of permanence for his poem, although, given
his obscurity at the time, the hope may seem tenuous at best. Boland,
who has a whole series of poems on objects and artifacts in her vol-
ume *Outside History* (1990), is more ambivalent about the artwork in
front of her. Since it represents, sitting on her father's desk as it does,
some unknown tale from family history, the loss of detail is a source
of longing as well as fascination. Her poem is no ode, but it stands as
a worthy companion piece to a poem that is.

PASTORAL

PASTORAL POETRY IS another instance of type over form. As with ele-
gies, the pastoral can take various forms and serve various purposes
from the funereal (in which case, it would be a *pastoral elegy*) to the
celebratory. We may see, in classical poems and their more recent
inheritors (recent as in sixteenth century), shepherds and shepherd-
esses. Or perhaps the people in the poem will be Wordsworth's rustic
country folk or Frost's solitary figures and couples in crisis. What lies
behind the pastoral, usually unspoken, is a sort of nostalgia for some
golden past (although we might give Frost or Ted Hughes a pass on
this aspect) of rural simplicity by urban dwellers. The poems are writ-
ten, after all, more often by a resident living in Athens or Rome or
London than by someone busy dodging sheep droppings.

So IS THAT IT FOR THE CATALOG OF FORMS? NOT EVEN CLOSE. OVER
the centuries, forms have come and gone and sometimes come again,
have jumped from one culture to another, have undergone changes.
We discussed the ballad and sonnet earlier, so you can add them to
your database of poetic forms. What we do well to remember is that,
far from being restrictive, poetic forms are rife with possibilities.
There are things you can do—and things you're freed from doing—by
choosing a sonnet rather than an ode, a triolet rather than a sonnet.
Just as the limerick lends itself to the joke and the haiku to the image,
every form lends itself to certain modes of expression. We should ad-
mire, beyond the technical mastery, the wisdom of choosing a partic-
ular form when a poem seems to do its job well.

11

Shapes of Things to Come

───

ONE OF THE MOST DEMORALIZING PROSPECTS FOR A READER IS page after page of unbroken verse. We see several hundred lines marching down the pages without even the saving grace of a paragraph break and our hearts just sink. Okay, my heart sinks. I know this because for years I confronted *The Iliad* at least once a year, and for all that I liked the experience, getting started on each of those books that crept up near a thousand lines was almost more than I could bear. But it was ultimately okay, because the nature of epic narrative is such that one really doesn't have to lean in hard on analysis. Lyric poems, now, are a different proposition.

What are the alternatives to walls of unbroken verse? Stanzas. Strophes. Verse paragraphs. By "stanza" we mean a grouping of lines that will be repeated throughout a poem or section of a longer poem. "Strophe" and "verse paragraph" are largely interchangeable terms that indicate the number of lines may change from one group of lines to the next. Let's start with the regular one.

First, a question: How long is a stanza? Well, how long do you need it to be? For practical purposes, the utility of a stanza seems to break down after ten lines or so. Since I never shy away from pushing things to their illogical extreme, what good would it do to have a thousand-line stanza? In epic poems, that would be called a book, and repeating that precise number of lines would be meaningless, since who would bother to count them? At the other end of the spectrum, a one-line stanza is equally useless, since it allows for no pattern. So between greater than one and fewer than many, what configurations make enough sense to actually occur in nature? Moving from smaller to larger, we have . . . .

- **Couplets** are not often set off as stanzas of their own, but they have been much loved at various times in literary history, particularly in the eighteenth century of John Dryden, Alexander Pope, and Jonathan Swift. Rhyming couplets are also favored among purveyors of comic verse in most periods.
- **Tercet**—three lines, the most famous of which is *terza rima*. They can have other uses, but Dante has largely dictated how they will appear. Their other important use is in the *villanelle* form, as we have seen.
- **Quatrain**—four lines, with a variety of rhyme schemes, the most common being ABAB and ABBA. Since it is the nearly perfect length for conveying a single thought, it is probably the most used stanza form.
- **Quintain**—rarely used as a form, the term is even rarer. Five-line stanzas will commonly contain unrhymed lines or will carry rhymes from one stanza to the next. The lack of symmetry, which seems an impediment, can sometimes be liberating.
- **Sestet**—six lines, reasonably common, and not only for sonnets. Sestets can be employed simply as the equivalent of paragraphs in a long poem, or the constituent element in the *sestina*, as we saw in the previous chapter.
- **Rime royal**—seven lines, first used by Geoffrey Chaucer in several poems, notably *Troilus and Criseyde*. The rhyme scheme is ABABBCC, and it can appear as a single stanza or two stanzas (ABA-BBCC) or even three (ABA-BB-CC).
- **Octave**—when speaking of sonnets; "ottava rima" is the more

common term, and it has a specific rhyme scheme, ABABABCC. With the couplet after three alternating rhymes, the form lends itself to punctuating statements, which has made it a favorite of mock-heroic poems. As the name suggests, this one came via Italy, specifically from Giovanni Boccaccio's *Decameron*, whose concept Chaucer would borrow for *The Canterbury Tales*. Other versions of the eight-line stanza exist, but this is the famous one.

- **Spenserian stanza**—nine lines, Edmund Spenser's gift to English verse that isn't *The Faerie Queene* (although it was first employed there). There are three features of note. First, the rhyme scheme is ABABBCBCC, so things interlock—somewhat. Second, the stanza is written in our very good friend iambic pentameter—except, third, the ninth line, which is iambic hexameter (six feet rather than five), called an *alexandrine*. It has been used by a number of other poets, including most of the British Romantics, but it is sufficiently uncommon that I never suspect its existence when I see more than four or five lines grouped together. It sneaks up on me.

- Ten-line stanza (and beyond)—they can occur, but they are sufficiently rare that no one has bothered to come up with a name, or have but it hasn't caught on. Beyond here there be monsters.

Each sort of regular stanza has a set of practices, precepts, or outright rules that govern its practice. Once someone—a Spenser, say—introduces a novel form, his version becomes the standard. The quatrain has escaped this fate largely because it is so ubiquitous that no one progenitor can lay claim to it; the poetic canon is therefore pretty well split among the various available rhyme configurations. Which is just another way of saying, it's all been done before.

But what about divisions that are irregular? We call those *strophes* or *verse paragraphs*, depending on who is doing the calling.

Strophe comes from odes, which in turn come from Greek drama's choral odes. Typically, the chorus engaged in a back-and-forth both literally and figuratively. As it debated a point, it moved in one direction and chanted the strophe. Then, having reached its end point, it moved in the opposite direction and gave out the antistrophe. Sometimes this to-ing and fro-ing would repeat; other times a resolution of sorts would be reached, and that was known as an epode. So: strophe, antistrophe, epode.

For some reason, students resist "strophe" in favor of "stanza," which is too bad. "Strophe" gets you off the hook for any expectations that the second one will precisely resemble the first. I, for one, appreciate any term that offers me wiggle room, of which I need all I can get.

WHAT HAPPENS WHEN STANZAS DON'T LOOK LIKE, WELL, STANZAS? When we hear "stanza," we have an image of a block of text, a sort of black rectangle occupying a chunk of the white page. But that need not be the case. A stanza structure can be perfectly regular not in itself but in the repetition within a poem, as Marianne Moore illustrates in a poem we glanced at earlier:

The Fish

> *wade*
> *through black jade.*
>   *Of the crow blue mussel-shells, one keeps*
>   *adjusting the ash-heaps;*
>   *opening and shutting itself like*
>
> *an*
> *injured fan.*
>   *The barnacles which encrust the side*

of the wave, cannot hide
   there for the submerged shafts of the

sun,
split like spun
  glass, move themselves with spotlight swiftness
  into the crevices—
   in and out, illuminating

the
turquoise sea
  of bodies. The water drives a wedge
  of iron through the iron edge
   of the cliff; whereupon the stars,

pink
rice-grains, ink-
  bespattered jelly fish, crabs like green
  lilies, and submarine
   toadstools, slide each on the other.

All
external
  marks of abuse are present on this
  defiant edifice—
   all the physical features of

ac-
cident—lack
  of cornice, dynamite grooves, burns, and
  hatchet strokes, these things stand
   out on it; the chasm side is

> *dead.*
> *Repeated*
>   *evidence has proved that it can live*
>   *on what cannot revive*
>   *its youth. The sea grows old in it.*

You will notice immediately that the stanzas have a distinctive appearance. When we see four-sided block stanzas, we kind of know what to do with them. But not so with Miss Moore's fishy verse. We have to figure out some new strategy. Not that that's hard. The stanza pattern is quite rigid: five lines in each one, with the first two lines rhyming with each other, as do the third and fourth. What, you didn't notice? That's the wildly different line length tricking your eye.

Two things are true about Moore's titles: (1) they often act as the first word(s) of the poem and lead into the thing that seems to be the beginning, and (2) they may have very little to do with the actual subject under discussion. "An Octopus," for instance, is really about a glacier with eight arms that she saw described in a National Park Service brochure as "an octopus of ice." That description seems to have led to the thought: You know, that's a perfect way to mislead my readers. Part of the fun of a Moore poem is getting disabused of our incorrect assumptions, or at least it is for her fans, of which I am one. Your mileage may vary.

That playfulness extends to her stanza construction. She is quite serious about the rules she sets for herself in this poem, but that doesn't mean she needs to seem serious. Here is the seventh and penultimate stanza:

> *ac-*
> *cident—lack*
>   *of cornice, dynamite grooves, burns, and*
>   *hatchet strokes, these things stand*
>   *out on it; the chasm side is*
>
> *dead.*

No, it is not customary to achieve one's syllabic ends by hyphenating words. On the other hand, there is no rule against it. Plus, it's just funny, as is ending the previous stanza with "of"—how many lines, much less stanzas, of poetry end with "of"? I'm not coming up with a lot of instances off the top of my head, one more element that makes Moore such a rare bird. It is important, however, to note that she is doing this irregular thing in the service of play and humor; she does it because it's funny.

And after all, why expend all that energy to come up with something new if it doesn't please you?

Is Verse Ever Really Free?

I N THE EARLY TWENTIETH CENTURY, A TERM CAME INTO
the literary lexicon that had never been uttered before:
"free verse." There were poems here and there that qualified
as free verse, or at least as someone making pretty free with
verse. Predictably, the French rode this new wave. Some of
their nineteenth-century versifiers of the Symbolist stripe—
Rimbaud, Baudelaire, Jules Laforgue—started horsing
around with poems that broke out of the customary patterns.

Then there was Walt Whitman. He didn't so much re-
ject received forms as establish his own, using as a model the
Psalms of the King James Bible, themselves efforts to imitate
Hebrew poetry. His example led the way for modern poets to
ignore convention, because he had given them a new, if un-
conventional, one. If you want someone to break rules, find
an American.

To understand this odd term and somewhat odd prac-
tice, let's clutter the field with two more. In the beginning
there was *closed-form* poetry, which is to say poetry with
pretty strict rules. You know, rules like, "Thou shalt end the
line after ten syllables," or "Rhymes shall occur at the ends of

lines at predictable intervals," or "Thou shalt have no form before this form." But you know what poets are like. Obstreperous bunch. Make them follow rules for six or seven centuries and they get restless, maybe even decide that rules are made to be broken. What would happen, someone might ask, if we loosen things up a little, maybe worry less about iambs and trochees, have lines of different lengths. What if we write poems, another might ask, more like music and less like rhythmic machines? Except that one isn't theoretical; Ezra Pound didn't actually ask it but rather stated it in "A Retrospect." Along with coconspirators Hilda Doolittle (better known as H.D.) and Richard Aldington, he came up with three rules for the new poetry, circa 1912:

1. Direct treatment of the "thing" whether objective or subjective.
2. To use absolutely no word that does not contribute to the presentation.
3. As regarding rhythm: to compose in the sequence of the musical phrase, not in the sequence of a metronome.

And by "metronome," of course, he meant "received meter." Out with marching iambs and trochees, in with more sinuous rhythms.

What if those questions got answered? What would it look like? What would we call it? One thing to call it, in opposition to the term we just employed, is *open-form poetry*. It's a good, solid, useful term, but like most things good, solid, and useful, sort of dull. Nothing like *free verse*. Nobody can resist "free"—not shoppers, not victims of scams, not theorists, and certainly not young poets who have been feeling constrained by conventions and rules. It's just that . . .

How free is free? At the extremity, free verse is simply prose: no rules, but any sort of musicality or compression is lost in the looseness of phrasing. And no one can say, a priori, how closely free verse needs to stick to metrical verse in order to still be, well, verse. There's the crucial word: "verse." We're not talking about free expression or free association or free speech. It's free verse, the latter word balancing the former, keeping it in check just as the first extends the possibilities of the latter. T. S. Eliot, sounding more like a building contractor than a poet, expressed the matter directly, "No verse is free for the man who wants to do a good job." William Carlos Williams added a similar perspective when he said, "Being an art form, verse cannot be free in the sense of having no limitations or guiding principles." Even Yvor Winters, that great curmudgeon of American poetry criticism, gave the form its due when he said that "the free verse that is really verse, that is, the best of W. C. Williams, H.D., Marianne Moore, Wallace Stevens, and Ezra Pound is the antithesis of free." In each of those statements the emphasis falls on the last name of this new form. Or constellations of forms, really, for every poet's free verse, and to a large extent every individual effort, is a new form, with no other example being quite like it.

That's all well and good, but what makes it verse and not merely free?

Rules. The difference between this modern innovation and traditional poetry is that the rules come from inside. A poet may, as we have seen with Marianne Moore's "The Fish," employ a strict syllabic arrangement of her own making. And even if she uses syllabics in her next poem, the chances that she will use the same pattern of syllables per line or even the same number of lines per stanza is something approaching zero. Why go over the same ground again?

I once heard the singer-songwriter Mary Chapin Carpenter say that every new guitar tuning suggested a new song. So, too, with rhythmic arrangements: every new one occasions a new expression, a new poem. If E. E. Cummings chooses to emulate the rapid fire of a revolver with "onetwo-threefourfive pigeonsjustlikethat," he has to decide why five shots and not six, as well as why "pigeonsjustlikethat" makes more sense as a single word and why the two portmanteau words are separated from each other by a space. Whatever the size and shape and arrangements of lines in free verse poems, the writer shapes, limits, and controls what she can say with every decision she makes. We do a disservice if we fail to notice those decisions or if we read the result as mere prose that has been chopped into lines.

In each of these cases, the limitations, while self-imposed, resemble the old rules by forcing the poet to find the music in the measure. This is the thing that eludes Robert Frost when he says that writing free verse is like playing tennis "with the net down": it's really more like playing tennis with a net you wove yourself.

Don't misunderstand. There are a blue million poems out there claiming to be free verse that are merely sloppy, undisciplined, self-indulgent, and lacking in coherent rationale as to formal principles. If any. Which is also true of closed-form poems. The world is chock-full of terrible writing, which will always overwhelm the other stuff. And not just by unknowns. My copy of *E. E. Cummings: Complete Poems, 1904-1962* is so huge that it could be used as the counterweight for a trebuchet. Its weight could be reduced by 40 percent (at least) by removal of the experiments that went awry; the reduction in scale would reflect a net gain for poetry. On the other hand there are long stretches of *The Prelude* and *In Memoriam A.H.H.* that Wordsworth and Tennyson could have neglected to write with no resulting damage to the works. And yet we wouldn't list any of these poets on the second string. Their work is magnificent. Most of the time.

Quality in poetry is never a reflection of the chosen form. It's far easier to write a lousy sonnet than a great one, and lousy is all most of us could ever achieve. But we don't blame "sonnets" when a bad example crops up. Nor should we blame "free verse" for the poor examples we discover. Poetry is poetry, free or not. It is good or not in each iteration, each individual poem. We can read, analyze, judge, welcome, reject, celebrate, and appreciate only the poem itself, not "poetry." And really, would you want it any other way?

12

Images, Symbols, and Their Friends

———————

WE'VE PUT THIS OFF AS LONG AS POSSIBLE, AND THERE'S NO WAY around it. When people say they don't like poetry, this is almost certainly the part they mean. It makes your head hurt. It gives me a pain in the neck. There's a near-universal response that can be written as a proof:

1. Poems contain symbols;
2. Therefore, symbols are poems;
3. Poets put symbols into their poems;
4. Symbols are confusing;
5. Therefore, poets want their poems to be confusing;
6. Alternatively, teachers invent symbols that aren't really there;
7. Symbols are confusing;
8. Therefore, teachers use "symbols" to confuse and control students;
9. Symbols give me a headache and make me feel inadequate;
10. Therefore, I hate symbols;
11. Therefore, I hate poetry.

Let's fix that.

If you're like the rest of us, you've lumped a bunch of things together under one heading, and the scary one at that. What we really mean is a whole group of things—yes, symbol, but also image, metaphor, simile, metonymy, synecdoche, trope, personification—that come under the heading of *figurative language*. For purposes of our discussion, let's think of all those things as variations of *word-pictures*. That, by the way, is another, very old form of figurative language, a *kenning*, or the Anglo-Saxon word form that is made by jamming two nouns together with some violence.

The first and most straightforward word-picture is the image, which at its most basic is simply, as English poet C. Day Lewis wrote in *The Poetic Image* (1947), "a picture made out of words." Oh, like we couldn't figure that out on our own, right? One thing used to create another, simple substitution. Think of our pal Shakespeare describing the aging man as a tree in autumn-turning-winter, "when yellow leaves, or none, or few, do hang." Now *that's* a picture in words. That's its first task. A bigger job is for that word-picture to act as the *vehicle* for metaphors or similes. When Homer, for instance, compares the onslaught of the Greek hero Diomedes to a river in spate (unstoppable heavy flooding), that river is an image, a picture in words, usually many words, that acts as the vehicle (the thing that carries the load).

How about if, instead of speaking of symbols and metaphors and so on, let's start with the concept that lies at the base of figuration: *deflection of meaning*. First, the big caveat: things in literature are, first of all, their literal selves. A frog is a frog. This is what Pound means when he says that a poem needs to work on the level of the person "for whom a hawk is simply a hawk." So let's remember always to acknowledge first of all that the tulip is indeed a tulip before we go running off to assert that it's really a fairy. Having established its tulipness, however, we can begin to investigate whether it is carrying some secondary meaning.

In Shakespeare's Sonnet 73, for instance, we need to *see* that tree in late autumn with only a few or maybe no leaves (lovely of him to give us options for how we envision that tree). That is our primary image. Even before the image has been presented, however, its meaning is deflected toward something else. He hasn't simply presented a tree or a time of year, but a time of year reflected in a man's time of life, "That time of year thou may'st in me behold." The most obvious sort of deflection is the simile, which holds up a large sign shouting "Comparison ahead" by using "like" or "as." Homer's flooded river is introduced as a comparison to the hero's onslaught, "since he went storming up the plain like a winter-swollen river in spate." Telegraphing this comparison was extremely useful to the listeners of the poem, since they had a tremendous volume of material to digest of an evening, during which many of them would be sliding further from sobriety. Best to make clear that the swollen river you're about to introduce is used for illustrative purposes and is not some new topic being injected. The middle of an epic recitation is no place for subtlety. The simile is not restricted to the epic arena, however. Robert Burns says in a famous poem, "My Luve's like a red, red rose," leaving readers in no doubt as to the comparison. Even with the change from oral to written verse, the nature of the simile remains straightforward.

That other notable comparison, *metaphor*, is by contrast subtlety itself. Here, the *vehicle* and the *tenor*, the thing to which the vehicle is being compared (and don't blame me: I. A. Richards came up with the term long before I was born). So what is a metaphor? Let's say it's a simile that lost its "like," which is sort of true. Metaphors lack the overt declaration that a comparison is taking place, which is what the "like" or "as" represents. That declaration is not really needed. Most of the time when we hear a metaphor, we don't even notice, as when we might read, "He was cut down in the bloom of youth." Do you stop and think about the comparison to a flower? Of course not.

Metaphors worm their way into our consciousness (see, there's one now) so that their first, overt meaning gets lost. If we consider Sonnet 73, there are actually three metaphors at work, one in each quatrain. The first, as we just mentioned, is the tree in autumn. The second is the coming of night, "In me thou see'st the twilight of such day . . . Which by and by black night doth take away." The final one involves a dying fire, "In me thou see'st the glowing of such fire / That on the ashes of his youth does lie." These comparisons all march to the same beat, namely that time has had its way with the speaker and now his time is almost gone. Metaphors can occur singly, of course, but here Shakespeare wants the emphasis he achieves by stacking them. In other words, writers are free to use them as (in)frequently as they wish, and good ones will always possess power.

Neither simile nor metaphor, we should note, need be momentary invaders. Whole poems can be and often are built around them. Lord Byron does just that in "She Walks in Beauty" (1813):

> *She walks in beauty, like the night*
>   *Of cloudless climes and starry skies;*
> *And all that's best of dark and bright*
>   *Meet in her aspect and her eyes;*
> *Thus mellowed to that tender light*
>   *Which heaven to gaudy day denies.*
>
> *One shade the more, one ray the less,*
>   *Had half impaired the nameless grace*
> *Which waves in every raven tress,*
>   *Or softly lightens o'er her face;*
> *Where thoughts serenely sweet express,*
>   *How pure, how dear their dwelling-place.*
>
> *And on that cheek, and o'er that brow,*
>   *So soft, so calm, yet eloquent,*
> *The smiles that win, the tints that glow,*
>   *But tell of days in goodness spent,*
> *A mind at peace with all below,*
>   *A heart whose love is innocent!*

Byron sets up his simile in the first two lines with the comparison to "cloudless climes and starry nights." From there, he returns repeatedly to the theme of light and dark. The best of dark and light, he tells us, meet in her face and eyes, but mellowed to "that tender light" imparted by twilight or lighted night that is washed out in the brightness of "gaudy day." The second stanza is taken up with how the interplay is perfectly balanced: one shade the more, one ray the less—that is, the tiniest tilt toward more darkness—would have "half impaired" that perfect balance ("nameless grace") between her black hair ("every raven tress") and her fair complexion ("or softly lightens o'er her face"). That sense of balance persists into the final stanza even as it recedes into the background, replaced by his extolling of her inner beauty. In the first line he mentions the (fair) cheek and (dark) brow, while in the third he gives us "The smiles that win, the tints that glow," leading him to the conclusion that her days are spent in goodness, that her mind is at peace, her heart innocent.

Whatever qualms we may have about Byron's aesthetic-moral equating of outward beauty with spiritual purity, we can have no doubt of his sincerity that this woman he has seen (by most accounts, his beautiful cousin-by-marriage whom he saw in a black dress with spangles) overwhelmed his senses. Happily, the vision did not strike him wordless; by the next morning, he tells us, the poem was written.

Compare this to Frost's sonnet "Acquainted with the Night," which we looked at in the chapter on rhyme. The speaker tells us that he met the darkness full on, experiencing its silences and its noises, its murk and rain, its furtive travelers, and the one point of light, that "luminary clock," that declared the time "neither wrong nor right." Until that statement, the poem seems merely to be about an inveterate nightwalker, but the introduction of right and wrong suggests something else, that perhaps the darkness he has encountered is as much spiritual as physical. Whether one accepts this reading or not, what impresses is that the sonnet never loses sight of its main idea of the speaker who has experienced the dark side.

What these two poems show us, beyond the fact that poetry, even at one or two hundred years old, can be entirely accessible, is how to take a simple idea and wring every bit of meaning from it. Both the thoroughgoing darkness of Frost's poem and the play of dark and light in Byron's exert a grip on their respective poems that never slackens. Rather, they animate and control the release of information. This technique of employing an extended metaphor as the overriding device for the entire poem is called a *conceit*. That term is usually defined to mean an extended metaphor, but we can apply it as well to Byron's simile; it's just that similes generally are less tenacious about hanging around. John Donne is responsible for two of the most famous poetic conceits. In "The Flea," the speaker tells his beloved that, since the flea has bitten each of them, thereby commingling their blood, they are already as good as married and should therefore consummate their relationship without delay. This is a prime instance of a *carpe diem*—literally, "seize the day"—poem, the end goal of which is almost invariably the bedding of the implied listener to the speaker's argument. His other conceit is the compass (geometric, not geographical), which he uses in "A Valediction: Forbidding Mourning" (1613) to promise his beloved as he leaves on a trip that, no matter how far he seems to range away from her, she is always the fixed foot of a compass to which he is merely the movable arm, seemingly free but always connected to that fixed point that is the beloved.

THERE IS SOMETHING ABOUT LOVE THAT SEEMS TO CALL OUT FOR this sort of extended metaphor. At one time, of course, the reason was the difficulty in writing directly about the act of love, although Edna St. Vincent Millay dispenses with any coyness in her Sonnet 42:

> *What lips my lips have kissed, and where, and why,*
> *I have forgotten, and what arms have lain*
> *Under my head till morning; but the rain*
> *Is full of ghosts tonight, that tap and sigh*
> *Upon the glass and listen for reply,*

And in my heart there stirs a quiet pain
For unremembered lads that not again
Will turn to me at midnight with a cry.

Thus in the winter stands the lonely tree,
Nor knows what birds have vanished one by one,
Yet knows its boughs more silent than before:
I cannot say what loves have come and gone,
I only know that summer sang in me
A little while, that in me sings no more.

Well, then. Not much question what this one's about. That frankness, especially from a woman, created firestorms about her work. But that's not our interest here. Okay, maybe just a little. What really matters is the past, remembered and unremembered. In the octave, the speaker fails to recall the roll of former lovers. She can't remember those she has kissed or with whom she has slept the night through; they have become ghosts tapping in vain at the window to be admitted. She only knows that they won't come again.

If the poem were eight lines long, we might conclude that it is mildly shocking (when first published in 1920) or titillating (now). But when it makes its turn for home in the sestet, we see that something greater than naughtiness has been going on. Millay goes all Shakespeare on us with her tree in winter and the vanished birds and silent boughs and lost summer that "in me sings no more." She was thirty-one years old. That's why we do well to think of the speaker of the poem as a fictive presence. As a side note, if she were speaking in her own person, she likely would have changed her young men to men and women, being rather catholic in her tastes. What matters for us here, though, is the way that the wintry scene of the sestet alters and amplifies the metaphor of the octave. These are not mere forgotten lovers but figures of a departed youth. This is an instance of a conceit that deepens and expands, as many of the great ones do, as it moves through the poem. Not bad, when it has only fourteen lines through which to move.

HAVING FORESTALLED THIS PART FOR SO LONG, WE NOW MUST GIVE in and talk about it. I have one thing to say: yes. Yes, that is one you just asked about. Yes, so is that. After all, why did you ask? Because you were pretty sure. And yes, you do too know what it means. *Symbols*. Can't live with 'em, can't live without 'em. Although Lord knows plenty of folks would like to try.

Similes and metaphors are pretty straightforward substitution of one thing for another. My love is like a red, red rose. Not much wiggle room there: love = rose. Aging person = tree in late autumn. In each case, one element is carrying the weight for another (that vehicle-tenor thing). With symbols, no such luck.

At bottom, a symbol is an object or action or phrase that stands for something beyond itself. That can be an idea, a state of being, a spiritual condition, whatever. So far, so good. Except that that "something" isn't one and only one "thing." If a deflective-meaning equation is a one-for-one substitution, we call that *allegory*, not symbolism. When we see the green light on Daisy's dock in *The Great Gatsby*, on the other hand, we know it stands for *something*, but what that something is may be in doubt. Every reader will come up with a meaning that probably won't match what it means for Nick Carraway, much less for Gatsby himself. That light contains a host of possibilities, many of which are not mutually exclusive: we may sense that it holds several meanings for us all at once. And we can do this with any famous literary symbol, from Melville's white whale to Huck's raft to Harry Potter's scar to Frodo's ring. Nothing to be frightened of.

YOU WANT SYMBOLS IN YOUR POETRY? TRY THESE: A FIELD OF HAY being mowed by a scythe, a woods on a snowy night, a rock wall being rebuilt by two neighbors, an abandoned woodpile on the edge of a swamp, bent-over birch trees, a forking path in a forest. And those are the product of a single poet, as you probably recognize. Frost draws them from the natural world, or the natural world reshaped by humans, if you prefer, but in every case they raise more questions about humans than about nature. Nor do they provide simple answers: each of those symbols points beyond its specific identity toward some more universal condition and hints at a small constellation of possible meanings. Do the birches suggest wistfulness at the memory of youth? The desire to explore the next world without leaving this one (which the speaker makes explicit when he says he would like to climb on "toward" heaven but be set back gently on earth rather than achieve his target)? The inability of vegetative or human objects to withstand the greater forces of nature? Some combination? Other meanings entirely?

Here's the maddening part: the choice is yours. Oh, you're limited by your own life and reading experiences, at least to a slight degree. I have found that my own readings change over decades as my own circumstances alter. And the text rules out some meanings. The bent-over birches are not telling us, "The Martians are already here" or "Save the Whales"; there is simply no support in the text for Martian whales. But even when we rule out all the deranged possibilities, there is still a fairly broad range remaining to us.

I remember in secondary school sensing the entire class freeze when the teacher asked, "What does that mean?" We *knew* that there was an answer, *the* answer in the teacher's edition, and guessing wrong would make us look stupid. Now, we didn't really know if that sort of answer was there or not, but we *knew*, you know? My guess is that the teachers knew that there were always multiple good choices. And that the ridicule came not from that side of the big desk but from ours. In any case, these days we trust readers more to make good choices, to develop readings that make sense for them while respecting the text, to ask good questions of the text—and the instructor, when necessary—so that their readings are informed, interesting, wise. Own your reading. It won't be quite like anyone else's, but that's okay. In fact, more than okay.

13

Right Out Loud

A FRIEND OF MINE RECENTLY SENT ME A LINK OF THREE GUYS RAP-
ping the General Prologue of *The Canterbury Tales*. It's pretty
great, although you're getting that from someone who knows way
more about Chaucer than rap. What's interesting is how nicely the
poem fits into the beat; the rappers don't seem to be straining at all,
which reminds us of a couple of things. First, what we know from the
oldest reports about poetry performance is that it was accompanied,
in pretty much every culture, by music of some sort even if that was
only percussion—you know, like rap. Or 1950s Beat poetry. Second,
Chaucer himself belonged to the oral tradition of performance and
was a part of the early era of English culture to marry that orality to
written texts.

Beyond that notion, namely that great narrative poems can be
adapted to contemporary forms, the incident gives us occasion to con-
sider poems composed not for the page, as is our experience with the
vast majority of verse, but for oral performance.

Once upon a time, if you were like me, you were compelled to
commit some poetic act to memory. It may have been a sonnet, or pos-
sibly the opening lines of Chaucer's General Prologue to *The Canter-
bury Tales* or "The Village Blacksmith." The sonnet, by contrast, was

invariably by Shakespeare, and the bit of Chaucer, with the cruelty of Advanced Placement teachers everywhere, was assigned in Middle English, "to get a feel for the language." And we wonder why memorization gets a bad name! Just to prove my point:

> Whan that Aprille with his shoures soote,
>> [When April with its sweet showers,]
> The droghte of March hath perced to the roote,
>> [Has pierced the drought of March to the root,]
> And bathed every veyne in swich licóur
>> [And bathed every vein in such fluid]
> Of which vertú engendred is the flour[.]
>> [Whose strength engenders the flower.]

I have provided a "translation," set beside the original, just so you can have a handle on meaning here. This chapter, though, is about oral poetry, and this poet, Chaucer, stands at the border where oral tradition meets "modern" written verse. As such, his was an art that both poet and audience understood should be given voice in public performance. For full effect, you're going to have to read it aloud, which is scary and slightly embarrassing for most of us. First of all, read it as if it's German, but with a slightly French accent. That means speaking what for us would be the silent terminal e in "shoures" and "soote" and "ende." And gargle those internal consonant clusters as in "droghte" that have gone hushed for us; just put the word in the back of your throat and let it rattle around back there a little bit. Most importantly, don't be shy. It's like Roy Blount Jr. said of imitating Little Richard: you have to be willing to cut loose.

If you do that, you will almost instantly hear the music in the lines. You can sing them or chant them or, like our Internet friends, rap them precisely because they are musical. Rhythmic. Melodious. Consider just that opening line, "Whan that Aprille with his shoures soote." The sibilance of "his shoures soote" just begs to be spoken aloud. The passage virtually sings itself. Although the lines generally have ten or eleven syllables, they read as a sort of tetrameter, some of it trochaic, some iambic, with anapests (or very weak iambs) thrown in, so that each line has four strong stresses, rendering it suitable for a rap.

IF WE LEAP FORWARD SIX CENTURIES AND CHANGE, WE AGAIN FIND written poetry that achieves its fullest form in oral recitation. Sometimes with jazz combo. Our cliché of beatnik culture involves goatees, berets, striped jersey cloth, finger snapping, and a really hip cat chanting his verse backed by brushes on a snare drum. No, it wasn't all like that. But there were times when it was exactly like that, which is where the cliché came from. And many of the Beat poets created poems for recitation, things that could only find their breathless quality when spoken by a voice struggling for breath. Like this:

> *I saw the best minds of my generation destroyed by mad-*
> *ness, starving hysterical naked,*
> *dragging themselves through the negro streets at dawn*
> *looking for an angry fix,*
> *angelheaded hipsters burning for the ancient heavenly*
> *connection to the starry dynamo in the machinery*
> *of night[.]*

Those are the opening lines of Allen Ginsberg's *Howl*, the poem that started that whole Beat mania. The poem maintains the breathless, headlong rush of this opening throughout. Hearing Ginsberg recite the poem—or even small pieces of it—the audience will inevitably wonder if he can possibly reach the ends of lines, much less the end of the poem, without some sort of collapse. Those first few words, "I saw the best minds of my generation," offers a false sense that the language will be somehow managed, controlled; instead, an ongoing eruption of language pushes that staid notion to the back of the room. The surge of words in "starving hysterical naked" or "angelheaded hipsters" or "ancient heavenly connection" drives the listener (and even the silent reader) inexorably toward the next line and the next and the one after that and ever onward. Ginsberg himself spoke of the poem as an experiment with the long line, with the line as a unit of breath, of which he was blessed with a considerable amount. In this regard he shares an interest with the "Black Mountain poets," those writers teaching at Black Mountain College, such as Charles Olson, Robert Creeley, and Robert Duncan, who began experimenting with poetic lines as "breath units," which is to say the number of words that could be uttered on a single intake of breath. Olson was a giant of a man, Creeley very much not, and their line lengths may reflect those differences. In Ginsberg's case, he clearly wants to push his lung capacity to the limit with these lines, which, like line three, can run to eighteen or more words and only occasionally end in full stops that would allow the reciter to pause for a complete breath.

This penchant for oral performance among the Beat writers was a regular feature among the poets, of course, and not only Ginsberg but others as well, such as his publisher, poet Lawrence Ferlinghetti, became nearly as famous for their readings as for their written work. The reading as event was de rigueur for the Beats. A figure as secondary as Brother Antoninus (William Everson) was a riveting reader in his fringed jacket and flat-brimmed hat even in his later years when Parkinson's gave his voice a serious quaver. Nor were poets the only showmen. Even the novelists got in on the act, as when Jack Kerouac appeared on *The Steve Allen Show* in 1959 to read the ending of *On the Road* to Allen's piano accompaniment. Kerouac and Allen would go on to record a full album of poems-with-piano-in-performance. The spectacle of the poet with jazz combo quickly became notorious and proved almost infinitely subject to parody, but seeing that television clip, which is widely available, or hearing those recordings, we cannot deny the excitement of the occasion.

That excitement explains the appeal of the *poetry slam* of the late twentieth and early twenty-first centuries. To get a sense of slam poetry, look up a video of Taylor Mali performing "What Teachers

Make," a surefire crowd-pleaser. Poetry quickly has gone from a written form whose performance is comparatively static to a lively, sometimes frenetic performance mode where the words on the page—if they exist at all—are likely secondary to how those words play on stage. Slam poetry shares many similarities with rap music: emphasis on heavy rhythm (not always dominant in the slam scene but likely to show up), insistence on authenticity, awareness of how words play in audience's ears, and acceptance of occasional technical raggedness. Perfection is less important than infectiousness. People who rarely read poetry sometimes get hooked on poetry slams; there are worse addictions. Does this mean that written poetry is in danger from this younger upstart? Probably no more than it has ever been. There is some evidence that poetry sales have fallen in the first decades of the century, but poetry has never been a profitable commodity. More like a prestigious loss leader for publishers and bookstores alike. Whatever the causes behind the sagging numbers, slam poetry is not likely to be the chief culprit. If anything, the enthusiasm it engenders is apt to bring in new readers for the more traditional mode.

What does all this tell us? Just that there is always a hunger to have a creator of art speak to us, to tell us things, to sing to us, to read to us, to recite to us.

WE'VE BEEN TALKING LARGELY ABOUT WRITTEN VERSE THAT SOMEtimes gets aired in public. But what about verse that was never written in the first place, that only ever existed around a campfire or in a mead hall, poetry for an illiterate audience? That doesn't make them nonliterary, you know. Just lost, in the case of the great majority of oral epics that either didn't get written down or whose written record (usually dating from several centuries after the original tellings) were somehow lost. These tales were typically vastly long, heroic tales of great events real or imagined (or a little of both) involving great fighters struggling against gods and monsters as well as other great fighters. How on earth did those ever come into being? How did performers remember their lines? And why tell these massively long stories in verse?

Let's start with the memory problem, which will take us a long way toward seeing the whole picture. So how do you remember an epic like *The Iliad* or *The Odyssey*, which can push beyond twenty thousand lines? Practice. Years and years of practice. The singers would have apprenticed as children and had only one career path. There are no reliable records from the Homeric period (roughly twelfth through eighth centuries BCE), but we do have indications from more recent oral traditions from the British Isles to the interior of Turkey.

Several elements assist that process of learning the texts and keeping—and, even more important, recovering—their place during performances. First, there is *rigid meter*, a strong and even inviolable beat in the epic line. In Greek epics that beat was dactylic hexameter ("DUM-da-da" repeated six times in each line), as I mentioned earlier. That meter has huge implications for performers and listeners alike. Just imagine, if you as the singer suddenly lost the beat in, say, line 17,201, you could be wrecked for the rest of the evening or at least until you could begin a new section.

Every tradition of oral epic poetry has features called *formulas*, by which we mean prescribed epithets and descriptions of characters and objects and gods. Athena is "gray-eyed" or "bright-eyed" or "of the gleaming eyes." Three ways to say the same thing? Why? We could say for variety, which would not be entirely wrong. But every epithet (or formula), and she had many others, has its own special rhythm, either coming in on the first beat of a metric foot or maybe the second or third, and walking out again on another specified beat of that or the next metrical foot. These exist chiefly to keep the beat going, but they have the secondary effect of letting the momentarily lost singer find his way back onto the beat.

Some formulas make sense to us today, but then there is "ox-eyed Hera," which throws us for a loop; even if we might regard eyes as large and round as a cow's the standard of beauty, we wouldn't express it in that way. On the other hand, the sixties brought us the phenomenon that was Twiggy, so maybe the Greeks were onto something.

When I taught *The Iliad*, I could count on questions as to why, for example, Hector was "of the shining helm" in one place and "giant, man-slaughtering" Hector in another, "glorious" in a third and "son of Priam" in yet another. And I would give them the answer, and before long someone would ask again. Sometimes with the very next question. Because they could not believe the truth. Being English majors or at least very well-trained readers, they were sure that they simply weren't reading deeply enough, that there was some secret meaning to choosing one or another of those descriptors for a certain passage. Because writers make these kinds of decisions to send messages.

And right there was their problem. Writers. *The Iliad* never had one of those. Instead, it grew in an oral tradition. We are so conditioned to imagine works of literature as products of a solitary mind at work in a lonely space that oral literature doesn't really make sense to us. Here's something like what happened with the Homeric epics. At some point after an event that may or may not ever have happened, at a place in Anatolia that may or may not have been Troy, a man (the one sure fact here, only because such performers were invariably male) who made his way in the world by singing for his supper created a long narrative song about the wrath of Achilles over the theft of his war bride by the Greek leader Agamemnon. As he repeated this performance in various banquet halls—because he was in all likelihood a traveling player—the story got more involved, more detailed, more fleshed out. And his apprentice, or maybe apprentices, would have learned the story, so when he moved out on his own, he took that one with him, along with a few other chestnuts guaranteed to warm Greeks' hearts after they filled their bellies with grilled ox and heavy wine. But, being his own man, he added more details and refinements to the song, and then he had apprentices, and they went their way, adding their own flourishes. In this way the tale grew and grew into the version that someone, when the system of writing came into being sufficiently to record it, wrote down what he had heard. The epic, as probably all oral epics did, grew over the course of several centuries by this process of aggregation and elaboration. But there was no "Homer" laboring away at a desk with a quill until the time for recited epics had nearly passed.

How can we be so sure that this is how the story came into being? Because at the time of the creation of this epic, the Greeks lacked written language as we know it. There is precisely one mention of writing in *The Iliad*. They did have access to a sort of record-keeping language called Linear B that was scratched into wet clay tablets with a stylus. It was a syllabic script—like Chinese, say—meaning that a character represented an entire syllable (eighty-seven in all). But what we know as Greek? They were no more able to read the letters on a fraternity house than we are.

But let's return to the main question: How could performers do this huge work and stay on task? Here are a few other elements, in addition to meter and formulas.

- **Repetition** (I). The poet-singer was a lot like the piano player in a bar at happy hour. Lots of people, many of them not on their first cup of wine, plenty of background noise. What's a poet to do? Repeat himself. Any important information or order is given three times. Zeus tells Iris, his messenger, to go tell Agamemnon to gather his generals. Iris duly conveys the message—word for word—to Agamemnon in his sleep. Agamemnon awakes and tells his brother, Menelaus—again, word for word—that he had a dream that he should gather the generals. It's fatiguing to read the exact wording three times, but it really works live.
- **Repetition** (II). Entire lines are routinely repeated, either exactly or with the name changed, as when we see two different men prepare for battle in exactly the same words. Anything to cut down on the need for on-the-spot invention.
- **Similes.** In this case, Homeric or epic similes. Some of which get pretty epic in their own right. When some important moment comes along, the poet describes it by means of a comparison to something natural—a lion stalking prey (a favorite),

a wolf, a bear, a flooding river, a field of wheat—that is then elaborated over multiple lines.

Since you probably lack the ability to read ancient Greek, and since I certainly do, it is impossible to show the metrical regularity of *The Iliad*, but we can look at some other elements. Here's the beginning of Book 10, in which Agamemnon sends Odysseus (who has his own epic, of course) and Diomedes, second in ferociousness among the Greeks only to Achilles, out on a nighttime spy mission that becomes, because Diomedes is involved, a killing spree:

> Now beside their ships the other great men of the
>   Achaians
> slept night long, with the soft bondage of sleep upon
>   them;
> but the son of Atreus, Agamemnon, shepherd of the peo-
>   ple,
> was held by no sweet sleep as he pondered deeply within
>   him.
> As when the lord of Hera the lovely-haired flashes his
>   lightning
> as he brings on a great rainstorm, or a hail incessant
> or a blizzard, at such time when the snowfall scatters on
>   the ploughlands,
> or drives on somewhere on earth the huge edge of a tear-
>   ing battle,
> such was Agamemnon, with the beating turmoil in his
>   bosom
> from the deep heart, and all his wits were shaken within
>   him.

Yes, we have formulas. Agamemnon is "shepherd of the people," Hera "lovely-haired." And repetitions. I think every insomniac in the epic is "held by no sweet sleep," while those more blessed have "the soft bondage of sleep upon them." Beyond that, he finds that "all his wits were shaken within him," a formulation that shows up over and over. The turbulence the king feels is compared in a simile to the storms that Zeus (he is the lord of Hera, of course) brings about when he fires off lightning at the earth. That particular simile is a mere four lines, not counting the thing being compared, Agamemnon's inner storm, which makes it just a baby in Homeric similes. All the same, there can be no mistaking what he is going through. The target audience may have been unsophisticated by our standards, but they lived close to the land and would have understood the full wrath of the storms described. Not only that, but they would have expected strong similes as an essential element of the heroic narrative.

Our language about poetry constantly reminds us that in the first instance it has always existed to be spoken and heard. "What do you hear in that line?" "The poet's voice is unmistakable." "He has a tin ear." "The last line echoes line two." "The poem speaks to us." As well it should. We want to have poems speak to us, to hear their music, to sense that voice. And history reminds us that even kings like to have poems spoken to them.

14

Bards and Beatles

—————

ERIOUSLY? SONGS? HERE TODAY, GONE TOMORROW? "SO ROLL OVER, Shakespeare and Whitman, to make room for the Monkees"? Not exactly where I was going, but since you mention it, we might want to remember that a modern troubadour named Bob Dylan won the Nobel Prize in Literature in 2016. And that the original troubadours, Arnaut Daniel and Bertran de Born and their many colleagues, were poet-musicians from Southern France who traveled and performed in the late Middle Ages. Seven centuries later Ezra Pound, no slouch himself, declared Daniel the greatest poet ever.

Besides, the Monkees wrote very little of their hit material. And most of those who wrote for them were excellent wordsmiths, including Neil Diamond and Carole King.

The first thing to admit is that songs generally follow the patterns for poetry in their language. In English, as we have long since established, that mostly means iambs and trochees, those two-syllable metric feet. How many-footed are those lines? Ah, that's where the art comes in. But songs also have ends of their own to pursue. In a form that passes by in mere moments, the hook, whether we speak of the rhythmic/melodic hook of the tune or the lyric hook, is even more important than in poetry. Try this:

The Mississippi delta was shining like a National guitar.
                        Paul Simon, "Graceland"

How can you resist that? My answer would be, we can't. Simon's cleverness at introducing the blues with the reference to National steel guitars, those inexpensive resonant instruments that were often all the early bluesmen could afford, along with the surprise of the simile using them as the basis for comparison to their homeland, the Mississippi delta, immediately captures our attention. Not every first line is as evocative as this one, although many aspire to such a state.

But even titles themselves can contain the promise of the poetry that lies beyond. Consider Willie Nelson's "Funny How Time Slips Away": we can all but hear the story that must go with that title, and the uneven meter—"Fún-nĭ hŏw tíme slíps ă-wáy"—suggests the spoken rather than sung element of the song. By contrast, Neil Young's "The Needle and the Damage Done" indicates a much more orderly rhythm, something almost approaching a march. And we are no less certain about the story to follow. In "Thunder Road" and "Born to Run," Bruce Springsteen signals the melodic and lyrical dynamism to come. "Over the Rainbow" suggests a dreamy, impossible quality, especially in the era before mass air travel, and the song delivers beautifully. True, many titles are deliberately pedestrian. Joni Mitchell's "Both Sides Now," aside from some shift of thought implied in the "now," gives little indication of the aching disappointment to follow.

Songs have always used poetry. The terms "verse" and "chorus" are impossible to disentangle from their poetic origins. "Verse" comes from the Latin *versus*," which meant "against" or "to turn," and was related to the act of plowing a field, where one turned at the end of each furrow. We should count ourselves lucky to get off with a mere five letters; the Greek equivalent was *"boustrophedon."* The chorus, meanwhile, had nothing to do with showgirls and high kicks, but was the group of men in a Greek play (standing in a circle called the "orchestra," by the way) who interacted with the characters and, to fill interludes when the characters were offstage, sang or rhythmically chanted the dramatic odes. Which of course constitute a type of poem.

Let's stop short, however, of the mists of time and settle merely in the dim past of folk songs. From 1966, to be precise, when Simon and Garfunkel used the second line of this song as the title for their album and set the song in counterpoint against Paul Simon's own composition "Canticle."

> *Are you going to Scarborough Fair*
> *Parsley, sage, rosemary and thyme*
> *Remember me to one who lives there*
> *She once was a true love of mine*

"Scarborough Fair" had been around for a very long time before Paul Simon learned it from English folk singer Martin Carthy, who got it from a songbook by Peggy Seeger and Ewan MacColl, who ultimately got it from a line of tradition stretching back several hundred years to Yorkshire, where Scarborough is located. Bob Dylan had already used the melody for his "Girl from the North Country." There, that ought to be enough legendary names for any discussion.

The song makes use of any number of poetic devices. First of all, musical settings enforce regular metrical patterns. In this case, the poem is written in four-beat lines that begin with trochees ("Áre yŏu," "párs-lĕy") and then switch late so that the lines conclude with iambs ("rŏugh fáir," "ŏf míne"). The lines sneak in a ninth syllable ("gó-ĭng tŏ" in the first line) and even a tenth or in one case an eleventh. You can get away with that easier in a song. And of course the ABAB rhyme scheme remains throughout. This is somewhat easier because the B rhymes are always the same: "thyme"/"mine." The thing that really catches our eyes—and ears, because this is a song—is that the second line of each stanza is always the same, "Parsley, sage, rosemary and thyme." It forms the first, unchanging, half of a refrain, the second half of which shifts from "She once was a true love of mine" to "Then she shall be a true love of mine" to "And she shall be a true lover of mine" to "Then she shall be a true lover of mine." Notice that in the last two the word "love" acquires a fifth letter, causing us to think about the difference between a love and a lover. This song is recognizably poetic in ways that one whose lyrics are chiefly "Baby, baby, baby, yeah, yeah, yeah" may not be.

So is this, a poem by William Butler Yeats called "Down by the Salley Gardens":

> Down by the salley gardens my love and I did meet;
> She passed the salley gardens with little snow-white feet.
> She bid me take love easy, as the leaves grow on the tree;
> But I, being young and foolish, with her would not agree.
>
> In a field by the river my love and I did stand,
> And on my leaning shoulder she laid her snow-white
>   hand.
> She bid me take life easy, as the grass grows on the weirs;
> But I was young and foolish, and now am full of tears.

Here's the thing about this poem: Yeats said he got it from an old woman singing a song of which she could recall only three lines, and those not precisely. Now, Yeats was fully capable of inventing the old woman, but there is in fact a traditional song, "The Rambling Boys of Pleasure," whose structure and wording are much the same. "Salley," by the way, is a word for the willow tree that no American has ever heard except in this poem. The poem is pretty straightforward: boy wants girl urgently, girl tells boy to want her less urgently, boy persists, overplaying his hand, and girl leaves boy grieving at his loss. It is a lovely poem, beautiful in sound and image, as in the simile, "as the grass grows on the weirs." There are few hard sounds, no g or k sounds, the two in that simile notwithstanding, in a poem dominated by sibilants and liquids. Consider the couplet, "In a field by the river my love and I did stand, / And on my leaning shoulder she laid her snow-white hand," with its f and v and l and r and s sounds. You could hardly find two softer lines if you hunted all week. Very, you know, lyrical.

All fine and good, but what does this have to do with songs?

Two things. First, if you cast your mind back to Yeats saying he got the idea from an old woman singing a partially remembered song, it began life as one. Indeed, his original title was to be "An Old Song Re-Sung." And second, several modern composers have put the poem to either existing tunes or their own compositions. Chief among them is that modern giant Benjamin Britten, who set the poem to music for his partner, singer Peter Pears. Performances of the song, including one with Pears singing to Britten's accompaniment, reside online. So we have pretty obvious connections between verse and melody in this case. Others of Yeats's poems have been set to music, notably his poem "The Second Coming" to a composition by Joni Mitchell, "Slouching toward Bethlehem," which can also be found online. This poem rests less comfortably in its musical setting than does "Salley Gardens," and Mitchell makes some editorial changes, although she's mostly faithful. The sonnet has some of Yeats's more vexing prophetic issues rattling around, and those cannot be heard and processed in the time they take to sing. After all, "Spiritus Mundi" (roughly "the world-soul") is going to be meaningless to untrained ears; it's bad enough in print. The amended result is jarring on first hearing for a committed Yeatsian, but that's my problem and likely not yours. What both of these settings point out is the way that a certain sort of traditional poem lends itself to melodic interpretation. It needs to be metrically regular, and easily grasped rhymes are a bonus; we expect our songs to rhyme. It helps if the concepts or imagery are not too challenging, which is why "Salley Gardens" is a happier marriage of music and verse than "The Second Coming/Slouching toward Bethlehem."

What is not necessarily an impediment are unfamiliar words. Consider the cases of two parties, one a professional poet, the other a troubadour, an itinerant performer. Both were inveterate collectors and shameless repurposers of folk melodies. Robert Burns (1759–96) could be classified as one of the earliest folk musicologists, roaming the countryside gathering melodies. Where lyrics existed, he insisted on maintaining the songs' tradition in the interest of something like cultural purity. Where no lyrics could be found, he provided them. As a result, the world now possesses not just "Auld Lang Syne" but also "Tam o'Shanter," "Ae Fond Kiss," "A Man's a Man for A' That," and this one:

> O my Luve's like a red, red rose
> That's newly sprung in June;
> O my Luve's like the melody
> That's sweetly play'd in tune:
>
> As fair art thou, my bonnie lass,
> So deep in luve am I:
> And I will luve thee still, my dear,
> Till a' the seas gang dry:
>
> Till a' the seas gang dry, my dear,
> And the rocks melt wi' the sun:
> I will luve thee still, my dear,
> While the sands o' life shall run.
>
> And fare thee weel, my only Luve
> And fare thee weel, a while!
> And I will come again, my Luve,
> Tho' it were ten thousand mile.

"A Red, Red Rose" is one of the famous ones, and for good reason. The poem itself is lovely and tender, and the melody, impossible to produce here but widely available online, is an ideal match for the lyrics, soft, soothing, assuring. If you must leave your love behind, as the speaker does here, best to do it gently. Not merely any red rose, the opening simile tells us, but one "newly sprung in June," which is to say one full of the promise of summer. More, that love is "melody" "sweetly play'd." What beloved doesn't want to hear that? He reassures his girl with promises, vowing "I will luve thee still, my dear" not once but twice, then transforming it to "And I will come again, my Luve" in the final stanza. His vows of steadfastness, moreover, are attached to the eternal, "Till a' the seas gang dry" (also twice), "And the rocks melt wi' the sun," and "While the sands o' life shall run." If you're going to promise unwavering loyalty, go big. We're not surprised, then, when he promises to return "Tho' it were ten thousand miles." The concepts are not difficult—we'll come back to that point in a bit—and they go in expected directions. "I will always love you," the speaker says, "till the seas run dry and rocks melt and the sands run out of life's hourglass." Any adored one will be hard-pressed to beat that deal. Not only that, but the speaker will find his way back, even if the distance were ten thousand miles—the equivalent of infinity to the earthbound traveler for whom a horse was fast transport. The dialect may give us difficulties, although fewer here than in some other Burns ditties, but we have no doubt as to the song's intent.

That's true also of the nearest thing to Robert Burns that America has produced, Woody Guthrie. Some of his lyrics have enough colloquial phrases and unfamiliar references to give outsiders pause, but they play just fine in performance. Besides, we're Americans, so the phrasing doesn't greatly boggle us. His most famous song employs a four-beat line to the tune of the Carter Family's "When the World's on Fire," itself quite similar to the Baptist hymn "Oh, My Loving Brother" (as a collector of melodies, Guthrie didn't balk too much at such fine points as copyright), and the beats aren't hard to find in the title, "This *Land* Is *Your Land*," and they continue their iambic march throughout. The words, on the other hand, are pure Woody.

The song actually has a great deal in common with "America the Beautiful." It takes this gigantic abstraction, *America*, and reduces it down to manageable images—first, California and Long Island, a state followed by a specific place within a state—and in doing so, he invokes both coasts, thereby encompassing the whole country pre–Alaska and Hawaii. From there he invokes the redwoods and the Gulf of Mexico, the long, thin strips of highway—quite new then—that crisscross the nation, valleys and wheat fields and deserts, even, in rarely performed verses, "No Trespassing" signs and relief (welfare) offices as indicators of class struggles in Great Depression America. Here's the thing about all of those specifics: they aren't. A cynic might ask, "Which desert, what valley?" But we aren't cynics here, right? After all, they are more exact than "This land." And Guthrie employs a trick that makes them seem more specific than they are: he puts himself among them. It is the speaker who is walking the roads from which he sees all these magnificent and sometimes lousy scenes. And then he repeats the first verse as a coda so that it has become for all of us who almost know the song the refrain. Then he, and later the Weavers, recorded only the first four verses and the coda. All very uplifting and positive. A folksy "America the Beautiful." After all, with their troubles with witch-hunting anti-Communists, the last thing they needed was more controversy.

But Guthrie wasn't writing another "America the Beautiful"; rather, he was fed up with hearing what he felt was the jingoism of Kate Smith's rendition of Irving Berlin's "God Bless America," which he felt entirely missed the point of the terrible state of the nation that had suffered through the Depression for a decade. He wanted to write a song that more accurately reflected the times, an effort in which the three sometimes ignored verses are critical. Of them, my favorite, because the most typical of Woody's humor, is the fifth verse. To look at a sign reading "No Trespassing," and realize that on the other side it says nothing and is therefore as welcoming as if there were no sign at all, is a near-perfect encapsulation of his subversiveness. Throw in the colloquial double negative (a Guthrie favorite), and you have him in a nutshell. He never says the sign was made for you and me, only the side with no writing. The final two verses, with mentions of relief offices and hungry people and the refusal to allow anyone to make him turn back on his march toward freedom, are straightforward attacks on the way the deck is stacked against the little guy. The fifth verse, on the other hand, is sly, which is when he's generally at his best.

Without Woody Guthrie, there is no Bob Dylan, or at least not as we have come to know him, so no Bruce Springsteen, no Joan Baez or

Willie Nelson or John Mellencamp or any of a thousand other singer-songwriters, not least among them Arlo Guthrie, which matters a lot, especially if you're Arlo. And without a thousand or so years of Western folk music behind him, there might have been no Woody Guthrie. There is a long tradition behind those songs that made their way across the Atlantic from Scotland and England and Ireland to New England and Appalachia and then to the hills of Oklahoma, where, he tells us, he was born.

HOW DO SONGS DIFFER FROM POEMS? THIS IS A GOOD QUESTION IN connection with Robert Burns and Woody Guthrie, both of whom preferred to write their lyrics first and then cast about for a melody to carry them.

- First of all, a song needs to be able to be sung. This assumes, of course, that you are not W. S. Gilbert, of "and Sullivan" fame, or Stephen Sondheim, of Stephen Sondheim fame. Both can be fiendishly difficult lyricists, often deliberately setting tongue twisters for their performers, as in the case of Gilbert and Sullivan's patter songs. For most lyricists, however, the primary interest is letting the singer actually get the words out.
- It also helps if the concepts are similarly straightforward, in which case "A Red, Red Rose" and "This Land Is Your Land" are each successful. So is "God Bless America," for that matter, which is why it was sufficiently ubiquitous to annoy Woody.
- They have to conform to their sound-shape, something poems lack. What I mean by sound-shape is that, while there is flexibility in numbers of syllables and so on, the stressed syllables have to be available to fall on the beat.
- At the same time, lyrics have less rigid requirements because syllables can be either crammed together on a beat (by replacing a quarter note with two eighth notes, for instance) or elongated across multiple beats. This sort of motor-mouth syllable

packing occurs in all sorts of comic songs, from Gilbert and Sullivan patter songs to music hall ditties of the early twentieth century to Warren Zevon's "Werewolves of London."

- There may be a need for a different meter for the bridge, if it is vocal rather than instrumental. This was not a problem for either Burns or Guthrie, as folk songs rarely have bridges, but it is a problem for modern popular songs, in which the bridge is often a striking departure from the parent tune even though it resolves back into the dominant key and rhythm for a return to the verse and chorus.

- Collaboration is encouraged. Naturally enough, lyricists often work with composers, which explains why "Hammerstein" falls so naturally after "Rodgers" or "Bernie Taupin" after "Elton John." Music guys and word guys are only occasionally the same guys; *The Wizard of Oz* needed both composer Harold Arlen and lyricist E. Y. (Yip) Harburg to achieve its magic. Their "Over the Rainbow" has been voted the greatest song of the twentieth century by more than one panel, and it is hard to imagine the century without it. But it is not uncommon for songs to have multiple lyricists or for rock tunes to be group efforts. Poetry? Not so much. Western poets have never been big on sharing.

As with excellent poems, there is a sort of inescapability to excellent songs from whatever era. Here's the chorus of something you might know, an instant classic from 1892 called not what you think but "Daisy Bell":

> *Daisy, Daisy, give me your answer do.*
> *I'm half crazy, all for the love of you.*
> *It won't be a stylish marriage,*
> *I can't afford a carriage,*
> *But you'll look sweet upon the seat*
> *Of a bicycle built for two.*

And just what is inescapable about it? Oh, any of a dozen things. The rhymes both at line ends ("marriage"/"carriage") and interior ("sweet"/"seat," "Daisy"/"crazy") are a good starting point. The way the lyric nestles into the melody—something impossible to render in print, of course—that makes it a classic earworm, one of those songs that starts playing on an endless loop in your brain. If you ever knew this song as a child, you'll be cursing me sometime in the next three days for bringing it up. In short, it does what a song is meant to do.

Or we could try something slightly more modern:

> *The long and winding road that leads to your door*
> *Will never disappear, I've seen that road before*
> *It always leads me here, leads me to your door.*
> *The wild and windy night that the rain washed away*
> *Has left a pool of tears, crying for the day*
> *Why leave me standing here, let me know the way.*

Even if you're not a Beatles fan, you won't be surprised to discover that the song is called "The Long and Winding Road." Like "Daisy Bell," it was an instant classic, the Beatles' twentieth—and last—number one song. Even the wall-of-sound meddling of Phil Spector couldn't wreck it, although it did neither the song nor Paul McCartney's performance any favors. The first thing that stands out—indeed, leaps off the page—is the audacity of the simple AAABBB rhyme scheme, and especially the re-use of "door" in lines one and three and "away" and "the way" in lines four and six. Who does that? Who can? If that showed up in an introductory poetry workshop, the instructor would likely tell the aspiring writer never to do that again. Here, however, McCartney proves that you can break any rule if you're good enough. Which he is. Notice, too, the softness of the consonants, the wealth of *w, l, r, s, n,* and *m* sounds. The *c* in "crying" after the *caesura,* the punctuation break, in line five is almost the only hard sound of the lot. And the imagery of the song, both the road to the door that has proved elusive and the rain-tears-pool imagery, is captivating. The song, which appeared in May 1970, nearing the end of a long, winding decade, felt like the end of something, as it proved to be. By the end of that year, the Beatles were legally dissolved as an entity. So we shouldn't be surprised that both the tune and the lyrics had a wistful, almost grieving tone. Or that they worked so beautifully together. It is one of the great Beatles songs; it is one of the great songs. Which means it refuses to be ignored. Few of us who encountered it on first release would rank it as our favorite of the group's efforts, but even fewer would dismiss it from the pantheon of their work.

Great songs are always great. That's why "John Barleycorn," which wryly follows the progress of barley from seed to plant to whiskey and goes back to at least the sixteenth century, can be picked up by the seminal British folk band Fairport Convention in the 1960s and from there find mainstream distribution via the progressive-psychedelic-jazz fusion rock band Traffic. Every new performer finds something a little different in it, and it nearly always sounds inevitable in the hands of good performers. Hearing Traffic's version, we think it's as if it were written for them, and this is why Steve Winwood's voice exists. Even if we thought the same thing of Fairport Convention's recording. And great songs find singers and audiences across centuries. We won't be around to experience it, but in a hundred or two or three hundred years, someone will find a reason to sing "Scarborough Fair" or "The Long and Winding Road" or "John Barleycorn," possibly in musical forms not yet imagined, and it will be fresh and new all over again.

Please don't misunderstand: the vast majority of popular songs are junk, as is the vast majority of everything, including poetry; the latest iteration of "baby, baby, baby, please, please, please" will be gone as fast as it came, a greater boon to humankind in its departure than in its arrival. At the same time, there is a lot of lousy poetry in the world—in every age—and we don't dismiss all poetry because of its worst practitioners. So let's not dismiss all song lyrics, either. Somewhere out there is a Yip Harburg or a Joni Mitchell, someone to help us imagine a place over the rainbow or a way to see clouds from both sides now.

Why
Is
Poetry?

15

Wanted: A Few Good Martians

MARTIANS? REALLY? YES, REALLY. ONCE UPON A TIME, YOU SEE, there was a poem called "A Martian Sends a Postcard Home" (1979) by Craig Raine. The poem takes an old philosophical notion—describe X from the point of view of a visitor from Mars with no knowledge of the goings-on of earth—and breathes new life into it. Such an idea lay behind a good deal of popular as well as philosophical culture. The screwball comedies of the 1930s often relied upon the main character not understanding how, say, life in high society worked, a trope that found its final resting place in television's *The Beverly Hillbillies*. The Clampetts may not have been from Mars, but in Beverly Hills, the Appalachian backwoods were a suitable substitute. Even earlier in the decade of Raine's poem, Robin Williams mined the earthbound-spaceman trope for comic gold in *Mork & Mindy*. Raine's gamble wasn't that his concept was too far beyond readers but that it might seem less than exotic. Or compelling. In any case, no worries. The key to his success lies in the crispness of his Martian's observations, and in the odd mix of worldliness and naïveté, as in the opening lines:

> *Caxtons are mechanical birds with many wings*
> *and some are treasured for their markings—*

they cause the eyes to melt
or the body to shriek without pain

I have never seen one fly, but
sometimes they perch on the hand.

There's a bit of trickery here at the beginning: How does the spaceman not know the word "book" yet know Caxton, the man who brought the printing press to England? It is more than many of my students knew, so discovering that the wings were pages and the mystery items books frequently came as a complete surprise. Later, the Martian can say that "Rain is when the earth is television," yet he doesn't understand the telephone, a "haunted apparatus" that people talk back to sleep when it cries and yet sometimes awaken "by tickling with a finger." Sketchy knowledge is sometimes a wonderful thing. Nor does he understand the purpose of a bathroom, which he believes is a place of punishment, given the noises people make there, noting that "everyone's pain has a different smell," perhaps the most thought-provoking description of defecation ever written.

Raine has no intention of making his Martian consistent. He is not a little green man, still less Marvin the Martian of Warner Bros. cartoon fame, but rather a conceit, a figure of dislocation and bemusement running through the poem. That's why, in a poem that begins with incomprehension over books, he can close with metaphorical reading:

At night, when all the colours die,
they hide in pairs

and read about themselves—
in colour, with their eyelids shut.

What really motivates Raine in the poem—in all his poems, really—is not space travel but *defamiliarization*. This is a term coined by Viktor Shklovsky in 1917 for a process we might call "making strange," or taking commonplace elements of our experience and making them alien to us, as if we never saw them before.

There are many ways a poet may make things strange. One, obviously, is the Raine path: take familiar items and self-consciously make them alien to us. It's a small school, but he is hardly the first nor the last. Membership in the actual "Martian School" was mostly limited to him and Christopher Reid, with a handful of ancillary figures. But we can go back to the Romantic era, to William Blake, who didn't need to make things strange because he *was* strange. Most who know his name do so from "Tyger, tyger, burning bright, / In the forests of the night," but he can go so much further than that. In his visionary and prophetic poems he can be nearly impenetrable even two hundred years later. Later avatars might include Edgar Lee Masters, whose *Spoon River Anthology* consists of dramatic monologues by the residents of the Spoon River Cemetery; the mostly French and Spanish adherents of *surrealism*, which got strange pretty fast, but also American poets influenced by surrealism such as Robert Bly and John Ashbery, as well as Deep Image poets such as Diane Wakoski and Clayton Eshleman, and Ted Hughes, whose nature is never warm and fuzzy.

In general, this defamiliarization splits in two main ways: seeing things differently and saying things differently. Both paths are legitimate responses to Ezra Pound's dictum, "Make it new." Nor are they unrelated. Poets who would teach us to see anew must find language appropriate to that challenge. To go back to Raine, his Martian struggles for apt comparisons, having so few options. Mars evidently has birds, for instance, but no books, television but not rain, dreams but not sleep. Hey, it could happen. What always matters in the "magical alien" narrative is that the outlander knows just enough about what he sees to be able to comment, but never so much as to understand the things he comments on.

"Saying things differently" may sound redundant: Who among us wishes for more literature that states things exactly as they have always been stated? Exactly right. But this aspect of making it new encompasses a sizable range of activities. At the micro level, it can simply mean finding new arrangements of words that are specific to the individual poet's immediate task. There may be only so many ways to speak of being in love, but that doesn't stop songwriters from trying to get beyond "moon"-"spoon"-"June" rhymes—even when they use them—to find unique ways of expressing that love. The eighteenth-century poet Alexander Pope said of "true wit" that it involved saying "what oft was thought but ne'er so well express'd," meaning that it dresses commonplace thoughts up in unique garments. That's not our understanding of wit, which generally involves being funny (something to which he was not opposed), but it covers our discussion of poetic originality pretty well. Wallace Stevens would be a modernist inheritor of the Pope mentality. At the end of "The Man on the Dump" he asks the question, "Where was it one first heard of the truth? The the," thereby becoming possibly the first poet to end a poem with "the," and certainly the only one to end with two. This is almost a perfect illustration of that definition of wit: even if we have considered the importance of the definite article relative to "truth," we almost certainly have never thought of abstracting the "the" out as Stevens does. That last line typically prompts a moment of befuddlement followed by another of illumination.

Consider, for instance, the problem of running out of fresh ideas. This situation is the source of nightmares for all sorts of creative types—artists, writers, performers, directors, teachers—for whom the terror lies in the possibility that their last inspiration may already be behind them. But it may apply as well to nearly everyone whose thoughts seem to have dried up, who may be left with nothing to say but a litany of worn-out expressions. So here's the question: Faced with this calamity, how does one write the next poem? How many ways can you say, "My thoughts have all dried up"? And the answer is, one more. For the elderly William Butler Yeats, tired and ill and intellectually stymied, the period of stagnation led to a startling image, that of himself as a ringmaster accustomed to marshaling his images, which were so many trained performers, around the circus ring. What came of that image was "The Circus Animals' Desertion," one of his greatest late poems:

> *I sought a theme and sought for it in vain,*
> *I sought it daily for six weeks or so.*
> *Maybe at last being but a broken man*
> *I must be satisfied with my heart, although*
> *Winter and summer till old age began*
> *My circus animals were all on show,*
> *Those stilted boys, that burnished chariot,*
> *Lion and woman and the Lord knows what.*

That's the first stanza, written in *ottava rima*, that gift to poetry from Giovanni Boccaccio, just to show that he'd lost none of his mastery of form, even if ideas had given him the slip. The rhyme scheme is pretty easy, the first six lines interlocking ABABAB and the last two forming a couplet, CC, and it had been around for about six centuries when Yeats used it. Here, he lays out his problem succinctly in the first two lines, that he had spent six weeks searching in vain for "a theme" or, in other words, a poem to write. This is a recent development, he says; until old age wrecked his abilities, his "circus animals," which he sketches in the last two lines, "were all on show."

In the next three stanzas of this three-part ode (although he avoids the term), he specifies the highlights of his career, from his early play *The Countess Cathleen* to his various uses of the mythic Irish hero Cuchulain, concluding with a remarkable statement, "Players and painted stage took all my love, / And not those things that they were emblems of." That confession, so stated, brings us up short: the poet so caught up with his art that for him real life was never *quite* real. It is at once somewhat shocking and inevitable; of course, we think, and how terrible. And with it, he gives us the liberating example that even great poets end sentences with prepositions.

In the third section of the poem, like the first a single stanza, he considers the source of that vast array of images and characters that propelled his career. Where did they come from? he asks, deciding that they emanate from decidedly unlofty materials, "A mound of refuse or the sweepings of a street, / Old kettles, old bottles, and a broken can, / Old iron, old bones, old rags, that raving slut / Who keeps the till." In other words, the detritus of life from broken pots to crazy people in shops, with a special emphasis on items that can be recycled. The metal objects were sold on to be melted down and recast, while bones went into the manufacture of soap and rags into paper. We have forgotten in the contemporary world that the rag-and-bone man was a regular fixture of cities a century earlier. Poets, this poet says, are also rag-and-bone men, scraping together the discarded, the unwanted, the unloved to make not soap or paper but art. An intriguing notion in itself, it leads to a closing image that is astonishing. "Now that my ladder's gone," he writes, "I must lie down where all the ladders start / In the foul rag and bone shop of the heart." Nothing—not the desolate tone nor the images of despair—has prepared us for this statement. Aspiring to rise high (the ladder), the poet must instead lie down among the trash and debris, which moreover is not that of the world but of the heart. I had never pictured the heart as housing that particular chamber. Reading it the first time, I needed a while to process all that the image offered. Generations of students taught me that my response was far from unique; we're never quite ready for the genuinely original when it appears. After all, where was it we first heard of the truth?

Finding ways to say differently is sometimes not a matter of elaboration but of stripping down. When the Imagists of the nineteen teens wanted to eliminate excess rhetoric from poetry and take it down to its essential elements, they went very short:

> *The apparition of these faces in the crowd;*
> *Petals on a wet, black bough.*

That's it. This Ezra Pound gem is probably the definitive Imagist poem. What makes it so is the juxtaposition of two seemingly unrelated elements with nothing more than a semicolon. No explanation, no apology, nothing. Oh, there is a title, "In a Station of the Metro," which is a help, especially once we know that the Metro is the Paris subway. From there, we can at least have a bit of context for the crowd. But what are we to make of those faces, or rather the "apparition" of them, and the petals plastered to a tree branch to which they are conjoined only by a bit of punctuation? Pound's answer is, make of them whatever you wish. He simply brings the two elements together, trusting his readers to find meaning for themselves. The customary reading goes something like this: the speaker, having emerged from the underground platform to the upper world of the station (Pound has said as much elsewhere), suddenly encounters the faces of the crowds of people, which seem to him in the first moment ghostly and in the second like so many petals of blossoms pasted to a tree bough. Your reading, as I've said before, may differ. What matters for our purposes is not the specific interpretation that you or I may impose on the lines but how Pound leads us to whatever conclusion. He says in an essay on poetry that it must make every word count. In a poem of this brevity, of course, that would seem to go without saying, but he really makes his words carry a load. The first noun, "apparition," is unexpected: How often in your reading has that been the first substance word you encounter? And when we find that it refers not to ghosts but to faces in a crowd, that pulls us along. The line is quite different from, say, "The crowd milled about the station and their faces shone." Less prosaic, more mysterious. Making the turn into the second line, we expect a payoff. We have been able to see that there are only two lines, and we know the rules: line two is supposed to make sense of line one in *some* fashion. What we find may seem to thwart our expectations, especially at first. It is a concrete image using concrete words: "petals," "wet," "black," "bough." Even so, it does not address questions that we've carried over from line one. We *see* the branch; we may not see the connection. We will, in the fullness of time, but time is required to fully digest this tiny poem.

Seeing differently and saying differently, as we might guess, are not mutually exclusive. Some poets manage to do both in some poems. When they do, the results can be spectacular. *The Waste Land* may be the most famously difficult poem in the language, even after a century. How much truer was that when it appeared in 1922? Readers had no context for something like this, with its vast web of allusions, borrowings, and outright thefts from other poems, its nightmarish vision of a civilization on its last legs, and its myriad voices. Worse, all the connective tissue had been removed. Imagism had ushered in a *poetics of disjuncture*, in which no context or exposition accompanies the poem. Of course, that's easy when your poems are five lines long: just the image, and then get out. Eliot, on the other hand, was writing a poem of 434 lines, a length where readers had learned that connections would be made. Suddenly, here's this poem that jumps from one thing to the next with no warning, no apologies, nothing but a line break:

> *"You know nothing? Do you see nothing? Do you remember*
> *"Nothing?"*
>
> *I remember*
> *Those are pearls that were his eyes.*
> *"Are you alive, or not? Is there nothing in your head?"*
>
>   *But*
>
> *O O O O that Shakespeherian Rag—*
> *It's so elegant*

So intelligent
"What shall I do now? What shall I do?"
"I shall rush out as I am, and walk the street
"With my hair down, so. What shall we do tomorrow?
"What shall we ever do?"

We shift suddenly from a series of complaints and accusations from a female speaker (reportedly taken from an actual conversation with his troubled wife, Vivienne) to an apparent non sequitur reply borrowed from *The Tempest* to a ragtime appreciation of Shakespeare and back to the existential angst of the first speaker. How do we get from "You know nothing?" to "that Shakespeherian Rag" and then back to "What shall we ever do?" The simple-minded answer is, the poem simply jumps from here to there and back again, and for once the simple-minded answer is right. The poem makes these astonishing leaps from idea to idea and language to language and says, in essence, come along and make of it what you will.

A crowd crossing London Bridge is described in words lifted from Dante, "I had not thought death had undone so many." The crowd is not dead, but the Great War is only four years behind the poem, and the casualty toll of that coupled with the influenza epidemic of 1918 mounted to somewhere in the neighborhood of forty million persons. There would not have been a soul crossing that bridge who was untouched by death. Eliot, however, leaves all of this background unspoken. We bring to it what we can. His first audience would have immediately grasped the war's impact, whatever else remained obscure; a century on, those associations have become more difficult. Even so, the poem invites us to collude in creating meaning. So we fill in some gaps, stumble over others, and perhaps fall headlong into those we cannot leap across.

The world Eliot describes is sullied, damaged, laid waste in ways that we might not have noticed before. At the same time, it presents the history of that world as simultaneously present: Queen Elizabeth and the Earl of Leicester glide along the same Thames as the modern watermen and slimy-bellied rats, while Dante, Shakespeare, and Charles Baudelaire are available to hold conclave with the Buddha and Tiresias and to provide commentary on the denizens of the local public house. Without doubt, that sort of simultaneity presents a challenge in its own right. The poem's main trial, however, lies in the utterly novel mode of presentation. Our first encounter with *The Waste Land* reveals a poem like no other; we might read for a thousand years only to discover that the poem's uniqueness remains. And having read it, for the first or fourth or fiftieth time, our view of the world and of the possibilities of poetry will never be the same. We see and hear and speak differently.

And really, you already know that is part of what we hope poetry will do for us.

Conclusion

Supreme Fictions

THIS IS BASED ON NO SCIENCE, PSEUDO OR OTHERWISE, BUT I firmly believe that the elapsed time between the development of language and creation of the first poem was about five minutes. I heard opera star Renée Fleming the other day saying that music may have developed even before language, and it seems reasonable to me. Humans have an innate impulse toward expression, and what is more expressive than music, however rudimentary? It's tempting to argue further that, having discovered music, humans set about making words so that their tunes would have a story, so that George Gershwin would have his Ira, but it seems more likely that language came about so that someone could trade these six colored stones for those ten seeds, so I'll not make that argument. Besides, I'm pushing my luck already.

When we speak of poetry, we can mean narrative or epic (the latter a subset of the former), dramatic, or lyric, but since the lyric has been the chief focus of this discussion, let us continue in that vein. Of those three classical genres, the first two have something, story, that the third lacks. Which is where we must begin our investigation for what makes poetry so compelling. It is, you know. Compelling. Why else have kings and queens kept pet poets to sing of their achievements when mere scribes could have recorded events just as well? Why have societies valued poets laureate to commemorate the good and terrible moments, the births of princelings and the sinking of fleets? Why do even those who have no regular truck with poems find it somehow ennobling when one is read at an inauguration or a commencement or a funeral? Why, for that matter, do so many students who never read poetry nevertheless undertake to write it? Take it from me: their numbers are legion. Even those such as Ben Lerner who would glibly write about and claim to share in *The Hatred of Poetry* can't stop speaking of it. If it is so terrible, why not simply leave it alone? Why return to it time and again? Why? Because there is something poetry can do for us that no other written form can do.

Only . . . what is that thing?

We know it isn't story; we already conceded that point. A handful of lines, even a handful of pages, won't be able to recount *War and Peace*. Nor do they try. When Tennyson writes his "Ulysses," he skips over the vast tales of war and vexed travels to focus instead on aftermath: the dissatisfactions of the adventurer in old age becalmed in domestic waters, seeking still to satisfy the will "To strive, to seek, to find, and not to yield." Shakespeare's Sonnet 73 tells us not of the whole arc of growing old but of the moment in which he speaks, when one's awareness of death's approach moves from hypothesis to certainty: "This thou perceivest, which makes thy love more strong, / To love that well which thou must leave ere long." No, poems are not all about growing old. Just the great ones. Taken together, these two poems, which *are* about growing old, reveal one of the sources of the lyric's power.

Moment and mood and melody. If narrative and epic are movies, to use a latter-day analogy, the lyric is a photograph. It may be a snapshot or an Ansel Adams landscape, but it is a single picture. A sonnet is a lousy venue for a story, but it's great at capturing an instant. As well as the response to that instant. When Seamus Heaney writes of the Northern Irish Troubles, he does so not by covering the broad expanse of civil strife but by zeroing in on moments: an assassination on a dark road, a retaliatory bombing, a stray word or phrase, an ancient person discovered in a bog whose form reveals some aspect of the Troubles. The insights he offers are not into matters of policy or strategy but into being. Which is to say that he explores matters not of social organization but of the spirit.

This is what Wallace Stevens means when he speaks of poetry being a "supreme fiction" in his poem "Notes Toward a Supreme Fiction." What Stevens suggests is what poetry has always suggested in hints, whispers, and shouts: that the poetic reality stands as an approach to God for the religious or a replacement for the unbeliever. Stevens's supreme fiction is that presentation of reality (which he always insists upon as the basis for imagination) that ripples with a sense of rightness, a vibration at the proper frequency.

Having been fairly nuts-and-bolts until now, I hate to go all mystical and ephemeral on you now, but it is mystical. And ephemeral. If you reach out to grasp it, your hand goes right through nothing to the nothing beyond it. If you close your eyes and wait, that nothing becomes a something, however inchoate. Stared at, it vanishes. Small wonder, then, that the Romantics' favored emblem of the poetic imagination was the aeolian harp, that strung box played only by the movement of the wind across the strings.

Ephemeral, too, is the whole enterprise. Most readers will never meet the creators of most of the poems they read nor the creators the vast majority of their readers. For one thing, the relationship is carried on not only across space but across time as well, and we can never meet Blake or Sappho or Whitman. Perhaps that's for the best, that poets remain for us spectral presences hidden safely behind their works. Worse, a poem has almost no value in a material culture. Few poets have ever made a living from their artistic creations and so have fallen back, depending on the era, on the patronage of wealthy benefactors (or, more precariously, of kings and queens), or academic positions, or jobs as editors, translators, bankers, radio presenters, insurance attorneys, or pediatricians. A lucky few, such as James Merrill, have had inherited wealth behind them, and one or two have farmed or raised horses. Some have lived as itinerants, visiting various towns as paid performers, troubadours or minstrels, or, like Dylan Thomas, performers of their own and others' works. More than a few have lived on the edge of poverty. Or even over the edge. And yet every age has produced—and continues, and will continue, to produce—persons willing to court financial ruin in the pursuit of poetry.

Why? Because they can't help themselves. It isn't simply that they need to say something; rather, something needs to be said, to find expression in this moment in a way it has never been expressed before. Like the ministry, it is a vocation, a semidivine calling to a task the undertaking of which, minus that calling, is irrational. That calling may be spiritual, as with the Romantics or their later relatives such as Gary Snyder or Merwin or even Sylvia Plath, or it may be messianic, as with the activist poets who would educate or lead us, from the Puritans to the Black Arts Movement poets and even including those like Adrienne Rich or Eavan Boland, whose work stands as a corrective to the male-dominated verse of so much poetic tradition. In any case, the call is made; the vocation comes because the voice has spoken. Poets don't choose; they are chosen. Now, they may choose to decline the honor, but they do so at the peril of their mental health. Of course, that peril exists as well for those who accept.

Who are they, the ones who accept the vocation, perhaps against their better judgment? By way of answer, let's consider two poems, both from early volumes by their writers, just about a century apart.

The first is William Carlos Williams's "The Great Figure" (1921):

> *Among the rain*
> *and lights*
> *I saw the figure 5*
> *in gold*
> *on a red*
> *firetruck*
> *moving*
> *tense*

> *unheeded*
> *to gong clangs*
> *siren howls*
> *and wheels rumbling*
> *through the dark city.*

The second, by Danusha Laméris, is called "Before" (2014):

> *The table still set.*
> *The goblets filled with wine.*
> *Her body lean, taut as a birch.*
> *The gifts not yet given.*
>
> *That which will be torn remains whole.*
> *The heart, unbroken.*
> *The mother alive, setting out the dishes.*

Each poem does remarkable things with time. Williams suspends it, as if this dervish is captured in a freeze-frame so that it moves down the street in a whirl but moves down the page a word at a time, "moving / tense / unheeded." That "tense" cuts two ways, suggesting the apprehension of those on board and "tensed" as in coiled for action as if it were a spring. The previous two-syllable line, "moving," is even more telling. Written as prose, those three unpunctuated words, "moving tense unheeded," would suggest a jumble of frenetic action, but isolated on its own line, "moving" is not moving. It is isolated both from its subject ("firetruck") and its modifiers ("tense / unheeded"). Curiously, this freeze-frame manages to suggest a cinematic quality, something many writers sought in the wake of that new technological marvel, film. In this case, the fractured sentence flow suggests the montage, a series of very brief shots separated by equally quick cuts and relying on nothing more than juxtaposition and the viewers' ability to assemble the fragments into something meaningful.

Laméris achieves something equally remarkable, invoking an unspoken "After" to match the titular "Before," simultaneously holding the future at bay and pitching us forward into it. The table is "still set," suggesting that it will soon be otherwise; "the heart [remains] unbroken," which guarantees that it will not stay thus. Most chillingly, "The mother [remains] alive, setting out the dishes." The final lines rely on our understanding of parallel construction with the first line of the second section to convey the sense of impending doom, and we have no choice but to comply. Her little poem is like a novel in miniature: just the hint of a story arc full of suffering and loss contained in the gem of a "still" moment in time. This is what poems can do, contain multitudes in miniature.

So how did they fare, these two early volumes? Williams's *Sour Grapes* (1921) was largely unnoticed by critics, although the always-perceptive Kenneth Burke got what Williams was aiming for in a review in *The Dial* in 1922. While the volume is not a classic, it contains several, including "Queen-Anne's-Lace," "Complaint," and "A Widow's Lament in Springtime" as well as our poem. *The Moons of August* was Laméris's first book, published by Autumn House Press as the winner of its annual poetry contest. It received several positive reviews, most notably from Naomi Shihab Nye. Whether any of its poems will become classics is beyond our ken, but it contains numerous powerful and intriguing poems, which is a good start.

These two poems express the principles of moment and mood and melody as well as any we might choose. In their compressed field of view, they suggest events far beyond their scope. Where is the emergency that propels the fire engine? Why is it unheeded in its headlong rush through the city? What is the tragedy that awaits this family after this meal? What are the sources of heartbreak? The poems, being something other than journalism or fiction, don't tell us. To give us the full story, Laméris would be writing *To the Lighthouse*. But she isn't; she is writing "Before." And Williams isn't bringing us the news; he's bringing us a stilled-life, a snapshot of a moment on the way to becoming news. Both direct us to bring our own imaginations to bear on the materials of the poems. They cannot be read without application of our creativity to that of the poets. They are, in short, the "supreme fictions" that Stevens esteems, the candles throwing their light high against the dark wall of experience. The set table and the rushing fire truck take their places alongside Keats's Grecian urn and Wordsworth's ruined abbey as occasions to explore the divinity of experience and the miracle of imagination.

Poems Cited

Anonymous, *Beowulf*
Anonymous, "The limerick packs laughs anatomical"
Basho, "An old silent pond"
Katharine Lee Bates, "America the Beautiful"
William Blake, "The Tyger"
Robert Burns, "To a Mouse"; "A Red, Red Rose"
George Gordon, Lord Byron, "She Walks in Beauty"
Lewis Carroll, "Jabberwocky"
Geoffrey Chaucer, *The Canterbury Tales*, General Prologue
Samuel Taylor Coleridge, "Kubla Khan"; "This Lime-Tree Bower My Prison";
    "The Rime of the Ancient Mariner"
Billy Collins, "Sonnet"
E. E. Cummings, "anyone lived in a pretty how town"; "Buffalo Bill 's"
Harry Dacre, "Daisy Bell"
Emily Dickinson, "Because I could not stop for Death"; "'Twas later when the
    summer went"
Paul Laurence Dunbar, "Compensation"
T. S. Eliot, *The Waste Land*
Stephen Foster, "Oh, Susanna"
Robert Frost, "Acquainted with the Night"; "The Road Not Taken"; "Birches";
    "Mending Wall"
W. S. Gilbert, "I Am the Very Model of a Modern Major-General"
Allen Ginsberg, *Howl*
Woody Guthrie, "This Land Is Your Land"
Thomas Hardy, "Birds at Winter Nightfall"
Seamus Heaney, "Bone Dreams"
Homer, *The Iliad*
Gerard Manley Hopkins, "The Windhover"

Langston Hughes, "The Negro Speaks of Rivers"; "Mother to Son"; "The Weary Blues"

John Keats, "Ode on a Grecian Urn"

Danusha Laméris, "Before"

Philip Larkin, "Church Going"

Edward Lear, "There Was an Old Man with a Beard"; "The Owl and the Pussycat"

John Lennon and Paul McCartney, "The Long and Winding Road"

Henry Wadsworth Longfellow, *The Song of Hiawatha*, "Hiawatha's Departure"

John McCrae, "In Flanders Fields"

W. S. Merwin, "Early One Morning"

Edna St. Vincent Millay, Sonnet 42 ("What lips my lips have kissed")

Clement Clarke Moore, "A Visit from St. Nicholas"

Marianne Moore, "Poetry"; "The Fish"

John Newton, "Amazing Grace"

Edgar Allan Poe, "The Bells"; "The Raven"

Ezra Pound, "In a Station of the Metro"

Craig Raine, "A Martian Sends a Postcard Home"

Christina Rossetti, "An Echo from Willow-Wood"

William Shakespeare, Sonnet 73 ("That time of year thou may'st in me behold"); Sonnet 30 ("When to the sessions of sweet silent thought")

Paul Simon, "Graceland"

Wallace Stevens, "The Man on the Dump"

Dylan Thomas, "Do Not Go Gentle into That Good Night"

Traditional, "Scarborough Fair"

Traditional, "The Yellow Rose of Texas"

Walt Whitman, *Song of Myself*, XI ("Twenty-eight young men bathe by the shore"); "Out of the Cradle Endlessly Rocking"; "O Captain! My Captain!"

William Carlos Williams, "The Great Figure"; "The Red Wheelbarrow"

William Wordsworth, "Tintern Abbey"; "My Heart Leaps Up"

William Butler Yeats, "The Circus Animals' Desertion"; "Down by the Salley Gardens"

Critical Works for Reference

You know how people say so-and-so has forgotten more about a subject than most people will ever know? That's not me, but I have forgotten more poetic thinking than I ever knew. But that's okay: sometimes it comes back to me little by little. The list below is a small portion of what I once knew. Or maybe it is everything and I flatter myself among all that forgetting. I let some writers and books stand in for a number of others, as when I use Cleanth Brooks as the representative figure for all of those brilliant New Critics of the midcentury period whose students taught the students who were my colleagues and me. The point is that there are a lot more sources out there and these are by no means the last word on words. I have stuck to the twentieth and twenty-first centuries, although it pained me to leave Samuel Taylor Coleridge and Sir Philip Sidney on the sidelines. Take this list with a grain or two of salt: it is good enough, but you'll do better if you get serious about studying poetry. Go forth with my blessing!

Owen Barfield, *Poetic Diction* (Faber and Gwyer, 1927. He has bigger goals, but the one that most interests us is Barfield's notion that diction, word choice, and usage constitute acts of imagination to which attention must be paid. It isn't the place to start, but if you're serious about poetry, at some point you will come to him.

Harold Bloom, "The Art of Reading Poetry" (HarperCollins, 2004). One of the giants of literary study gives us a nongigantic discussion of reading poems in this introduction to his *Best Poems of the English Language*. He hits many of the important elements of poetry reading with his usual flair and erudition.

Eavan Boland, *Object Lessons: The Life of the Woman and the Poet in Our Time* (Norton, 1995). Every student of poetry should read Boland on the struggle of a woman to become a poet.

Cleanth Brooks, *The Well Wrought Urn* (Harvest Books, 1947). This is the work through which a great many of us met the full expression of the

New Criticism, with its insistence on staying inside the text and working closely, sometimes exhaustively, with the language of the poem. Under Brooks's influence, I once wrote four pages on four lines of Shakespeare, but Brooks should not be held responsible.

Kenneth Burke, *Language as Symbolic Action* (University of California Press, 1966). A lengthy collection of essays. Burke establishes that language is a particular form of action that works by displacement of meaning. He's a brilliant rhetorician and student of symbolism in its many guises.

John Ciardi, *How Does a Poem Mean?* (Houghton Mifflin, 1960). This is the work that taught a couple of generations of us that it isn't only what the poem means but also the means by which it creates meaning that matters. Still something close to the industry standard.

C. Day Lewis, *The Poetic Image* (Jonathan Cape, 1947). Perhaps the first really thorough analysis of its subject. And one of the last. It's really insightful.

Terry Eagleton, *How to Read a Poem* (Blackwell, 2007). Eagleton worries that careful, close reading of poetry is a dying art, and he plans to restore it in this witty, wise book.

T. S. Eliot, "Tradition and the Individual Talent" (1919; reprinted in *The Sacred Wood*, 1920). The famous study of how poets find their way into the pantheon, from a poet who intended to (and did) arrive there. He gives us the notion of the genuinely new work "taking its place among the monuments."

Seamus Heaney, *Preoccupations: Selected Prose 1968–1978* (Faber and Faber, 1980). I learned as much about poetry in a single afternoon with Heaney as in any graduate seminar I ever took. Heaney's essays (this is the first collection) are always wise and sharp, offering that same level of insight.

Geoffrey Hill, *The Lords of Limit* (Oxford University Press, 1984). I stole about half my chapter titles from his essays. Hill was a formidable, brilliant, difficult poet, and he's all that as an essayist, too, but well worth the labor.

Edward Hirsch, *How to Read a Poem and Fall in Love with Poetry* (Harvest Books, 1999).

John Hollander, *Rhyme's Reason* (Yale University Press, 1981).

Ben Lerner, *The Hatred of Poetry* (Farrar, Straus and Giroux, 2016). Well, why not? He's a poet himself, so much of his hatred is tongue in cheek, and he makes some good points in this small book.

Mary Oliver, *A Poetry Handbook* (Mariner Books, 1994). Oliver aims first of all at aspiring poets, but her insights are very helpful to general readers as well.

Robert Pinsky, *The Sounds of Poetry* (Farrar, Straus and Giroux, 1998). A slender book, it discusses exactly what it promises and does so beautifully. And Pinsky has the poetry credentials to back up what he says.

Mark Strand and Eavan Boland, *The Making of a Poem* (Norton, 2000. The subtitle is *A Norton Anthology of Poetic Forms*, and if you wish to know about how the important poetic forms work, this is the book for you.

Yvor Winters, *In Defense of Reason* (Alan Swallow Press, 1947). Winters may be the best reader of poetry who ever lived. From him, and him alone, I learned the notion of secondary stresses (that not all are created equal). He was also a cantankerous old devil, even when he was a young devil, and he raised literary invective to a high art. That alone makes him an interesting read, but you will learn so much from him that you'll be thankful you undertook the task.

Acknowledgments

No one can write about poetry without a great deal of help. Over the years, I have been blessed with great teachers and colleagues, many of whom were also excellent poets, and their insights and lessons have been invaluable. In particular, I am indebted to the late R. K. Meiners, Linda W. Wagner, F. Richard Thomas, and Leonora Smith of Michigan State University for their wisdom early and late, and to my colleagues and friends Stephen Bernstein, Danny Rendleman, Scott Russell, Jan Furman, and Fred Svoboda of the University of Michigan–Flint for their excellent thoughts and considerable patience with me on matters poetic. Above all, I am indebted to a generation or so of students whose questions, ideas, and occasional quizzical expressions have kept me up to the mark year after year. A special thank-you is due to Megan Riley for her assistance in the early research for this book. As ever, none of this would be possible without Brenda, who smooths the pathway and manages the annoyances so I have the liberty to be this silly. Finally, I wish to remember my first great teacher, friend, and classmate, Keith Bellows, who got me through the frightening two-term English literature sequence (unlovingly titled "*Beowulf* to Virginia Woolf" by the victims) at Dartmouth when I knew about as little as it was possible to know about poetry. Brilliant writer, fascinating raconteur, ferocious editor, he left us much too early. Without him, there is no chance that I would be here to write this book.

Index

Permissions

About the Author

THOMAS C. FOSTER, author of *How to Read Literature Like a Professor* and *Reading the Silver Screen*, is professor emeritus of English at the University of Michigan–Flint, where he taught a wide range of classes in fiction, drama, and poetry, as well as creative writing and freelance writing. He is the author of several books on twentieth-century British and Irish literature and poetry, and he lives in East Lansing, Michigan.

ALSO BY **THOMAS C. FOSTER**

HOW TO READ LITERATURE LIKE A PROFESSOR

A Lively and Entertaining Guide to Reading Between the Lines

Available in Hardcover, Paperback, E-book, Large Print, and Digital Audio

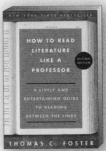

"A smart, accessible, and thoroughly satisfying examination of what it means to read a work of literature. Guess what? It isn't all that hard, not when you have a knowledgeable guide to show the way. Dante had his Virgil; for everyone else, there is Thomas Foster."

—Nicholas A. Basbanes, author of *A Gentle Madness*

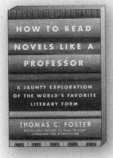

HOW TO READ NOVELS LIKE A PROFESSOR

A Jaunty Exploration of the World's Favorite Literary Form

Available in Paperback and E-book

Thomas C. Foster, author of *How to Read Literature Like a Professor*, returns with another lively literary guide, this time diving into the popular novel. Readers will gain insight into the hidden language of novelists and the keys to a more enriching (and fun!) reading experience.

TWENTY-FIVE BOOKS THAT SHAPED AMERICA

How White Whales, Green Lights, and Restless Spirits Forged Our National Identity

Available in Paperback, E-book, and Digital Audio

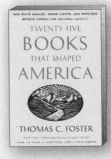

Thomas C. Foster applies his combination of know-how, inimitable wit, and analysis to look at the great masterworks of American literature and how each of them has shaped our very existence as readers, students, teachers, and Americans.

READING THE SILVER SCREEN

A Film Lover's Guide to Decoding the Art Form That Moves

Available in Paperback, E-book, and Digital Audio

Foster examines the grammar of film through various classic and current movies both foreign and domestic, with special recourse to the "AFI 100 Years-100 Movies" lists.

"[One of] this season's best books on Hollywood"
—*New York Times Book Review*

ML   3/2018